SECRETS ABOUT
LIFE EVERY
WOMAN
SHOULD KNOW

ALSO BY BARBARA DE ANGELIS, PH.D.

SECRETS ABOUT LIFE EVERY WOMAN SHOULD KNOW

TEN PRINCIPLES FOR
TOTAL SPIRITUAL AND
EMOTIONAL FULFILLMENT

BARBARA DE ANGELIS, PH.D.

HYPERION

NEW YORK

The author gratefully acknowledges permission to use the
following excerpts:

Excerpts from *The Subject Tonight Is Love: 60 Wild and Sweet
Poems of Hafiz* copyright 1996 by Daniel Ladinsky.

Excerpts from *Powerful Prayers* by Rabbi Irwin Katsof and
Larry King, copyright 1999 by Renaissance Publishers.

Excerpts from *Light Upon Light: Inspirations from Rumi* by
Andrew Harvey, copyright 1996. Reprinted with permission
of North Atlantic Books, Berkeley, California.

Excerpts from *Abandonment to Divine Providence* by Jean-
Pierre de Caussade, copyright 1975 by John Beevers. Used by
permission of Doubleday,
a division of Random House, Inc.

"Love After Love" from *Collected Poems 1948–1984* by Derek
Walcott, copyright 1986 by Derek Walcott. Reprinted by
permission of Farrar, Straus and Giroux, LLC.

"The love of God . . ." by Dante Alighieri from *The
Enlightened Heart* edited by Stephen Mitchell, copyright 1989
by Stephen Mitchell. Reprinted by permission of
HarperCollins Publishers, Inc.

ISBN 0-7868-8993-4

FIRST MASS MARKET EDITION

3   5   7   9   10   8   6   4   2

I offer these words to you,
my Beloved One,
who has opened the most secret doorway in my heart
and taught me the meaning of
true bliss, true peace,
and true love.

ACKNOWLEDGMENTS

I would like to express my love and gratitude to the following people:

To Bob Miller, my publisher at Hyperion: Thank you for having the vision to go in this new direction with me, for believing in my message, and for knowing our reunion was meant to be. I am glad to be working with you again.

To Leslie Wells, my editor: I am so grateful for your patience, your encouragement, and your gentle support as I went through the mysterious and challenging process of giving birth to this book.

To Harvey Klinger, my dear friend and literary agent: Thank you for knowing it was time for a change, and for waiting until I was ready. As always, you are in tune with my highest purpose, and I am so grateful to have you in my life.

To my assistant, Alison Betts: I am certain that God personally sent you to me! You nurture me, encourage me, keep my life running and keep my family happy so I can do the work I am here to do. I can't imagine having gotten through this year without you. Thank you for your unconditional love and for always coming from the heart.

To Ruth Cruz: Do you know what a difference you have made in my life? You have helped me serve so many people in your service to me and to those I love. You have a beautiful spirit and I know you are being blessed for your goodness.

To Pam Kear: I love you for holding my hand, drying my tears, cheering my breakthroughs, and always reminding me of the highest truth. Your friendship has been a harbor of comfort, healing, and strength for me, and I am so grateful for your loyalty, your companionship and your love.

To Tim Lehman and Vidura Barrios: I couldn't have a family any more wonderful than you. Thank you for taking care of me, for sharing your deepest hearts with me, and for treating me like a goddess. Your love always brings the highest truth along with it, as we see God in each other.

To my dearest friends Amanda Kamsler, Jackie Eckles, Kimberly Kerberger, and Lorin Roche: Knowing you were there for me allowed me to pass through some of the most challenging times of my life and emerge whole and triumphant. Thank you for always reminding me of what I deserve, and loving me no matter what I am going through.

To Margaret Sweet: Your gentle guidance has enabled me to be patient, persistent, and not give up hope. I am so grateful for the knowledge about the cosmos that flows through you, and for the clear and caring way you share it with me.

To Swami Durgananda: Your wisdom, your deep knowing, and your reassurance helped to hold open the door of transformation so I could walk through to the other side. Thank you, dear sister in spirit, for seeing where I was and what I needed, and guiding me with such confidence, compassion and certainty.

To Swami Kripananda: No words are adequate to thank you for the blessing you are in my life. I am in awe of the mysterious ways in which you serve as a messenger of grace, and I am humbled by your protection, your kindness, and your love. How grateful I am for your constant example of one-pointedness, surrender, and devotion, and for the tender yet unquestionable way you make sure I never waver from my one true goal.

And to you whom I was born to love: Know this book is dedicated to the miracle of our reunion.

CONTENTS

INTRODUCTION

The most auspicious moment of your life
is when you make the commitment to know the Truth,
a commitment so firm there is no turning back.

GURUMAYI CHIDVILASANANDA

I magine a life in which you woke up every morning excited about the day ahead and certain that, when you went to sleep at night, you would be able to say, *"This was a great day!"* . . .

Imagine knowing that no matter what challenges you faced in your relationships, your work, or your family, you would always remain centered, calm, and clear . . .

Imagine having a source of confidence and wisdom inside yourself that you could count on to be a constant wellspring of strength and inspiration . . .

Imagine what it would be like if you knew exactly what you needed to do to make each and every moment of your life one of great happiness, great contentment, and great peace . . .

The experiences I describe here aren't simply impossible dreams—they are possible, very attainable realities. They paint a picture of a life that, perhaps, has only existed as a dream you're sure could never come true. But it can. I wrote this book to help you create that kind of life for yourself, a life that feels like it is working, like it makes sense, and, most importantly, a life in which you are living and loving as the powerful, fulfilled person you've always wanted to be.

This book is about something every one of us seeks in our heart—true freedom, inner freedom, the kind that saints and mystics have written about throughout the ages. This kind of freedom is not the freedom to acquire more of what you can eventually lose, or to experience more of what will eventually change, or to do more of what will eventually not matter. Instead, it's the freedom that comes from knowing how to discover your own state of joy and contentment and protect it from all of life's ups and downs. It's the freedom that comes from knowing how to build a center of emotional and spiritual self-reliance on the inside, a center that will allow you to live every day with greater joy, greater strength, and greater peace. Most of all, it's the freedom that comes from finding a source of security and happiness inside yourself, happiness that nothing and no one can ever take away from you.

Ever since I can remember, I have been a seeker of this inner freedom. I've been on a conscious and committed journey trying to discover the truths about life that would help me make sense of my existence and get the most out of my time here on earth. At the age of eighteen, I found my first spiritual guide and since then, I've had the privilege of studying with many great and revered teachers and immersing myself in the knowledge and practices of the world's most ancient spiritual traditions.

Secrets About Life Every Woman Should Know contains the most important lessons about life that I have learned during my own profoundly transformative emotional and spiritual odyssey of the last thirty years. And even though the information in this book has been growing patiently and persistently inside of me for all this time, I couldn't have written it ten years ago, five years ago, even two years ago. Like a soup that you know still needs to simmer just a little bit more, this book needed these last twenty-four months of my life to add the final flavor. Now it's ready, and it is my privilege and great joy to be able to offer it to you.

All of us spend our lives searching, consciously or unconsciously, for lasting fulfillment. We make hundreds of decisions every day, from what to eat for breakfast to what CD to listen to in the car to how hard to work on a project to whom we fall in love with, based on what we think will make us happier, what will create a greater sense of security, what will provide us with more of the things we tell ourselves we need to feel successful and complete. Most of these decisions are an attempt to master, or at least cope with, the outer world. This is where we put our energies—trying to get what we want and keep everything under control.

In spite of our best efforts, in spite of how hard we try to get everything to turn out the way we want it to, a strange things happens: *our hopes and dreams keep bump-*

ing into reality. We have a picture of how we always thought our lives *should* be, but if we are really honest with ourselves, we have to admit that our lives look very different from that picture. And so we suffer, because what is happening is different from what we think *should* be happening, because we are feeling something different from what we think we *should* be feeling. Reality lets us down, not just once, but over and over again.

At some point in our lives, usually by the time we reach our thirties or forties, we face the difficult realization that *no matter what we acquire or achieve, we can't completely control what happens on the outside.* This conclusion often fills our hearts with a deep sensation of emotional and spiritual uneasiness, and haunts our minds with challenging and perhaps disturbing questions: **What is the purpose of my life? What am I supposed to be doing here? Why is it so difficult for me to experience true happiness, true inner peace?**

Have you ever seen one of those circus acts where someone has ten or twelve china plates spinning on top of thin sticks? The performer comes out and starts a few plates spinning and then adds a few more and a few more, until, hopefully, all his plates are spinning at once. At least, that's the idea. We all know what happens—just when he has the plates at one end of the table spinning right, a plate at the other end starts to wobble, so he runs down and gets it going faster. Suddenly, two plates in the middle look like they are about to topple off, and as soon as he sets them right, two others in separate spots are on the verge of crashing down. Back and forth he frantically races, the audience laughing with delight and cheering him on if he gets all of his plates to spin properly without disaster.

Why do we find this feat so fascinating? Why do we shriek with a kind of perverse delight when a plate drops? Because this display mirrors our own lives perfectly. The truth is, most of us live just like this. We have all these "plates"—our relationship plate, our work plate, our family plate, our money plate, our health plate, and so many others—and our goal is to keep them all spinning at once. You know what you did first this morning when you woke up? You mentally checked your plates!! *"O.K., the relationship plate . . . well, things with my husband are pretty good. How about the kids plate? Hmm . . . a little shaky. . . . Jennifer is having trouble in school, but it's not that bad yet. Let me look at this work plate. OH NO! It's wobbling pretty badly—I am really behind on that project at the office, and look down there at the money plate . . . Oh gosh, our credit card bills are way too high this month, that plate's about to crash . . ."*

And so you spend the rest of the day running around trying to get the shaky plates stabilized, and hoping that too many plates don't start to fall at once. Your idea of a "good day" is when all of your plates are spinning, no mishaps. And a bad day? Well, we all know what that's like: it seems like some devious, invisible hand is knocking one plate after another off the sticks, and no matter how hard you try, you just can't keep them up in the air where they belong.

This is the battle you face each day, the battle for

control of your life. You have your picture of how things "should" be, how your relationship "should" feel, how much money you "should" be earning, how your kids "should" behave, how people "should" treat you fairly, how it all "should" turn out. And when something happens that doesn't fit this picture, which it inevitably does, you feel like something is going "wrong"; you feel out of control. One of your plates has dropped. You may have been happy ten minutes before, but suddenly you're angry, or frightened, or depressed. *You have lost your state of equanimity.*

Like most people, I spent much of my life collecting what I thought were beautiful "plates"—the perfect career, the perfect relationship, the perfect home—then trying desperately to keep them all spinning, and praying none of them would crash to the floor. And of course I failed, because as we'll see later on, part of the purpose of life is for those plates to fall, and for us to learn the lessons that inevitably come when we are staring at the pieces of our egos scattered all over the ground. For me, each time a plate toppled over, I would feel as if somehow I'd done something wrong, and my inner state of peace and contentment would be shaken. *"If only I can get all my plates to stay up,"* I would tell myself, *"then I would finally be happy."*

It was my own fervent spiritual search for the truth that ultimately led me to a series of profound realizations. For over twenty years, I'd been teaching and writing about how to create loving relationships with the people in your life. There are emotional principles, I would explain, that make love work or not work, and if you take the time to learn about these principles, you will be able to experience more intimacy, more connection, more fulfillment. Eventually, I reached an even deeper level of understanding: the most important relationship I have, that we all have, is with life itself. I had patterns of relating to life—accepting it or resisting it, surrendering to it or misunderstanding it, approaching it courageously or approaching it fearfully, paying attention or ignoring its messages, being grateful for it or not appreciating its gifts—just as I had patterns in my human relationships. How I chose to interpret events that happened to me, the attitude I brought to each day when I woke up in the morning, the way I responded to difficulty, how much I listened to what my life was trying to tell me, all these habits were determining the quality of my relationship with life. And my relationship with life was affecting my relationship with everything else. It all started inside of me.

I knew the principles that made relationships work. I knew the principles that made communication work between two people. So what were the principles that could make my relationship with life work?

The Ten Secrets About Life

Secrets About Life Every Woman Should Know shares the answers I've discovered to these questions in the form of ten important principles, or secrets, about life.

These basic, universal principles have been taught and written about for thousands of years in all of the great philosophical and spiritual traditions of the world. Why do I call these underlying principles of life "secrets"? The English word *secret* is a word that comes from the Latin *secretus*, which means "hidden." These ten secrets aren't mysterious or hard to comprehend, *but they are ways of understanding life that have, indeed, been hidden from our awareness, and therefore whose wisdom we haven't had access to.* And as long as this wisdom remains a secret to us, we cannot benefit from it, and we go on living our lives feeling as if something essential is missing, yet not quite knowing what that is.

When you don't have the information about how to make something work, that thing becomes a source of frustration to you. For instance, no matter how wonderful your car is, if you didn't know how to start it, how to get it to move forward or to turn, you wouldn't be able to drive anywhere. If you bought an expensive, highly advanced computer but never read the manual or had someone show you how to operate it, the computer would just sit there on your desk, completely useless. A musical instrument like a piano or a guitar or a violin is worthless by itself—unless you know how to make it produce the sounds you want and then, it's magic.

This same understanding applies to your life. Like the car or the computer or the piano, your life will work or not work depending on whether or not you learn about the underlying principles or secrets that make life work. When we discover these principles and put them into action, it's as if we have suddenly pushed all the correct keys on the computer, or figured out how to put the car into the right gear. Everything begins to run more smoothly. Everything, finally, begins to make sense.

Here are the ten principles or secrets about life that this book introduces:

Secrets About Life

1. Everything you need to be happy is inside of you.

2. The purpose of life is for you to grow into the best human being you can be.

3. Change is inevitable, so stop resisting and surrender to life's flow.

4. All obstacles are lessons in disguise—honor them and learn from them.

5. Your mind creates your experience of reality, so learn to make your mind your friend.

6. Fear will steal your aliveness—make your courage bigger than your fear.

7. You must love yourself before you can truly give love or receive love from anyone else.

8. All relationships are your mirrors and all people are your teachers.

9. True freedom comes from how you respond to life and not from what life does to you.

10. Whatever the question, love is the answer.

Understanding these ten secrets has radically transformed my own life and the lives of many people with whom I've shared them. What I found is that, if at any moment I am unhappy, if I am upset or not feeling centered, if I have lost my sense of inner contentment and safety, it's because I'm violating one of these ten principles. I'm sabotaging my own happiness. And on the other hand, when I remember these secrets and put their lessons into practice, I feel powerful. I feel peaceful. I feel free.

What's exciting about the ten secrets is the astonishing revelation that *you already have everything you need right now to be happy.* There is nothing wrong with you that needs to be fixed; there is nothing missing in you that you need to find and replace. You actually don't need to add anything to who you are, but rather, to get in touch with what you already have inside of you. That's why this isn't a book about self-improvement—it's about self-discovery.

This is the essential message of *Secrets About Life*: that true emotional security cannot be found in hoping that our plates will keep spinning correctly, or hoping the sea of our lives will remain calm and no big waves will come and capsize our boats. The security we seek, the protection we long for, comes from creating an inner anchor, an inner self-reliance, so that no matter what happens on the outside, we remain firmly connected to a source of unlimited strength and peace on the inside. No matter what happens, we do not drown.

When the vision of Reality comes,
the veil of ignorance is completely removed.
As long as we perceive things falsely,
our false perception distracts and makes us miserable.
When our false perception is corrected, misery ends also.
SHANKARA

There are times in our lives when we really are ripe for growth. There are times when you are so ready to make a shift, that if you don't make it you become very uncomfortable. There are times when, if you stay where you are, you're going to suffer because you're not moving to where you need to be. If you're lucky, just when you start to feel you really do need to make a change, God, or the universe of Divine Intelligence, or whatever you want to call that greater power, places something in your path that is exactly what you need in order to take the next step. Maybe it's a person who inspires you to reevaluate yourself, or an experience that forces you to change, or a book that says just what you need to hear. These are magical moments when everything is in place, as if someone has arranged for you to see the picture of your life as it truly is, and suddenly the curtain goes up. And you look and you exclaim: *"Oh, my gosh, I didn't see this before."* The truth you see about yourself takes you to a new level of strength and power, a new depth of love and passion.

You're holding this book in your hands and reading these words because, whether you knew it or not, whether you expected it or not, this is one of those magical times for you. You are scheduled for a profound shift in your consciousness. Something wonderful is about to happen to you! Can't you feel it?

As we enter this new millennium, we are living in the midst of a very potent time ripe with opportunities for tremendous growth, tremendous awakening. It's as if a big wind is suddenly blowing through our lives, and that wind is the force of change, a benevolent, unstoppable force the purpose of which is to remove all those patterns and attitudes and old beliefs that are holding us back, and elevate all of us to a new, more expanded, and less fearful way of living. Have you noticed that wind beginning to blow on the inside and the outside of your own life? It has certainly been blowing strongly in mine, and I've also noticed this same process happening to almost everyone I know who is really sincere about becoming a more conscious human being. It's as if you have all the details of your life, your relationship, and your career all neatly and nicely stacked like an orderly pile of papers, and then, without warning, this huge breeze appears and blows all the papers up into the air. And you run around trying to pick up the flying papers and put them back where they belong, but the wind just keeps coming.

If you suspect that something has been stirring up your life, it has. It is the wind of change, the wind of grace. And if you listen carefully, you will hear it whispering to you: *"It's time for more joy and less suffering; it's time for more freedom and less fear; it's time to remember who you really are."*

This book is written in a woman's voice. It's not that these secrets about life aren't universal, or don't apply to men, for they do. But I wanted to offer this book as an invitation particularly to women, to my sisters in spirit, to invite you to share in the fruits of my own years of seeking and discovering. I believe that it is essential for us as women to teach each other, for when we honor the teacher in each other, we are then able to recognize the teacher in ourselves. I had so few female role models growing up, and my first guides, gurus, seminar leaders, mentors, and counselors were all men, which is the way it has been for so many of us. I feel honored that, in my work, I have been able to be a female guide for men and women alike, for I believe that something unique and magical comes through women when we teach others, and something is received that one cannot receive from a man—not something better, just something different. And yet, of course, this book is for men, too, and you will know just the ones with whom you need to share it . . .

Finally, *Secrets About Life* is a gift, not from me to you, but from you to yourself. You may believe you are reading this book because you think it might be interesting, or because a friend gave it to you, but I will tell you a secret: *you are holding this book in your hand because it is time for you to receive a gift, a gift from God or whatever force of grace you believe in.* Have you been asking for help in the silence of your own heart lately? Have you been praying for guidance? Have you been feeling you are ready to make a breakthrough? Perhaps the gift of information contained in these pages is what you're finally ready to hear. As the writer, I am just the person passing on the gift, as it was passed on to me. I invite you to read not only with an open mind, but with an open heart, and with the intention of receiving the messages that are meant just for you. Let the words penetrate deep into your being. Let them speak to your hungry spirit.

The great philosopher Plato once said that "the unexamined life is not worth living." The truth is, there's no greater gift you could give yourself than the time and the space to look within. There's no greater gift you could give to anybody else in your life—your partner, your children, your friends, your family, and even strangers. When you really look within, you will not be the same person when you bring your awareness back out again. Inside, there are such mysteries, there are such wonders, there is so much waiting to reveal itself to you. When you understand and work with these secrets, your ordinary moments can be filled with profound awakening and you can begin to live a life that gives you back all you hope for.

I invite you to walk with me and take the most important journey of all, the journey that will lead you back to the core of your self, the journey whose destination is an inner source of untouchable joy and contentment, the journey whose ultimate gift to you will be a state of true and lasting freedom. This kind of freedom is available to you right now, if you will only give yourself permission to experience it.

My dear one, are you ready to start living the kind of life you always knew was possible?

Offered with great love,

BARBARA DE ANGELIS

Everything
You Need
to Be Happy
Is Inside of You

Nothing can bring you peace
but yourself.

RALPH WALDO EMERSON

Let me tell you a story whose origins are from ancient India about the search for happiness:

In the beginning, God created the universe and all the people in it so that everyone was aware of his or her true oneness with God, and the great love within themselves. These were the secrets of life, and, after all, God loved everyone, so why not give them the greatest gift He could think of? Then God sat back and watched the play of life with all of its dramas unfold.

But as He watched, He soon realized something was very wrong. Whenever a human being met with a challenge, or went through tough times, the person would say to himself, *"This is awful. Why should I go through this? I am one with God, so I will just drop this human form and merge back into Him."* And that is exactly what happened. One by one, each human would remember his true self, and be unwilling to play the game of life.

God was very disturbed by this dilemma. The purpose of life was for these beings to learn and grow, not to bail out when the going got rough. So He called an emergency meeting of all the divine beings.

"After much consideration," God began, "I have decided that we are going to have to hide the secret of life, the secret of happiness from these humans. If they remember it, they have no interest in living an earthly life."

"But where will we hide it?" one divine being asked.

"Let's hide it at the top of the highest mountain on earth," someone suggested.

"No, that won't work," God replied, shaking His head. "Human beings are resourceful. They will find ways to climb up there and discover it."

"What about at the bottom of the ocean? They'll never go there," another offered.

"Oh, yes they will," God interjected. "They'll invent submarines. The bottom of the ocean won't do."

"I've got it!" said a divine being. "Let's hide the secret of happiness in outer space. Surely then it will be impossible for the humans to locate."

"But they will create spaceships and fly there," God sighed. "None of these suggestions will work. Still, there must be somewhere we can hide the secrets about true happiness."

"I know where you can hide it," a soft voice

replied. God looked up and saw a young, female angelic being He hadn't noticed before.

"Yes, my dear?" God asked. "Where do you think we should hide the secret?"

"Hide it deep within the human heart. They'll never look for it there."

God smiled, for He knew He'd found the answer. And then He made it so. And that's the way it has been ever since.

All of us spend our time here on earth searching for happiness, longing to discover the secrets for living a fulfilled and peaceful life. From our very first moments of existence as an infant until the day we die, we are motivated by the search for what we believe will make us happy:

"I want to be fed . . . I want to be held . . . I want to crawl over and look in that cabinet . . . I want that toy . . . I want to go to the amusement park . . . I want to stay up and watch TV . . . I want to get on the cheerleading squad . . . I want those kids to like me . . . I want that guy to be my boyfriend . . . I want to go to the mall and buy that outfit . . . I want to get into a good college . . . I want to lose these extra ten pounds . . ."

"I want him to ask me to marry him . . . I want to have a fancy wedding . . . I want to find the perfect apartment . . . I want to find the perfect job . . . I want to get pregnant . . . I want my husband to be more intimate . . .

I want to find a career that leaves me time for my children . . . I want to move into a bigger house . . . I want the kids to do well in school . . ."

"I want to have sex with my husband more often . . . I want the kids to go to college . . . I want my daughter to marry a nice boy . . . I want my son to stay in the family business . . . I want to take that trip to Europe we've always talked about . . . I want the kids to live close enough so we can visit the grandchildren often . . ."

"I want my husband to take better care of himself . . . I want to buy a condo in Florida for when we retire . . . I want to be well enough to attend my granddaughter's graduation . . . I want our investments to do well so I have enough money to live on if my husband passes away before me . . . I want to be able to have enough strength today to take a little walk . . . I want to see the ocean once more before I die . . ."

These are all lovely things to wish for. There is nothing wrong with these desires, or with the list you could write of what you believe would make you happy. But what happens inside of you when the things on your list don't come true? What happens in your heart when what you hope for in life doesn't happen?

You and I both know the answer to these questions: When we don't get what we want, we suffer. We feel disappointed, or angry, or hurt, or anxious, or insecure, or confused, or betrayed, and definitely *not* happy. *We have our list of expectations about life, about love, and we decide we are happy or not from moment to moment based on how many of those expectations are being met and how many are not.*

We go through this silent but deadly process of evaluating our happiness hundreds of times a day, perhaps dozens of times before we even leave the house in the morning. For instance:

Your alarm goes off and you are awakened from sleep. Another day has begun. So far, the day is neutral, neither a good day nor a bad day—just a blank slate. You open one eye to glance over at the window and see what the weather is like. It's raining. *"Darn,"* you think. *"Traffic is going to be terrible."* This is your first thought of the day. You have already decided that you aren't happy about something—the weather has not met your expectations and thus has disappointed you.

You roll out of bed and shuffle into the kitchen for your morning cup of coffee. Then you notice that your husband forgot to turn the automatic coffee machine on the night before, so there's no coffee ready. You sigh with annoyance. Expectation number two has not been met. You hear the kids stirring in their rooms, then determine that they are squabbling over who will use the bathroom first. Sigh again, this time with more irritation. *"Hey, cut it out kids—you only have a half hour to get dressed and eat before the bus comes, so move it!"* Good-bye to expectation number three, that your kids will calmly and quietly get ready for school without creating a fuss.

Back to your bedroom. Your husband is at the sink brushing his teeth. *"Good morning, honey,"* you say cheerfully, kissing him on the cheek. *"Morning,"* he mumbles back distractedly. You feel a painful tug in your heart, wishing he had greeted you with more affection, and as you wonder if something's wrong between you, your sense of well-being shrinks some more. You shower and dress. As you pull on your pants you notice that they seem tighter than you remember. *"Oh no, I have gained a few pounds again,"* you lament. Another expectation crashes down as it collides with reality. It hasn't even been an hour since you woke, and already you have collected enough evidence to make yourself feel some degree of discontent and unhappiness.

I am sure you have your own version of this scenario, your own list of unmet expectations which build up during a typical day or a typical week and put you into a less than happy state of mind. You think: *"If these things occur, I'll feel happy. But if these other things occur, I will feel unhappy."* I know I have an unconscious list like this; most people do.

The problem with these lists of expectations is that they set us up for inevitable disappointment. Why? Because life is unpredictable. No matter how hard we try to control people and events and circumstances, we fail. People don't behave as we want them to. Circumstances change that we'd hoped would stay the same. Events occur that are not in our control. As I wrote in the introduction, our spinning plates drop. Or, as a popular bumper sticker says, *"Shit happens."* And we all know it does.

What I've been describing is probably the most fundamental way you may be sabotaging your happiness in this life:

When you go through each day
expecting what is happening outside of yourself
to make you happy,
you are setting yourself up for failure.
You are setting yourself up for misery.
You make yourself a victim of circumstances
you cannot control
and become dependent upon others
for your own state of joy and contentment.

Why is basing your happiness on what's happening in your outer life such a spiritual and emotional dead end? *Because, ironically, when you count on the events of your outer life to make you happy, you are trying to create stability by clinging to that which is always changing!* By nature, everything in life is in constant motion. Nothing stays the same for long. So hoping to create peace and tranquility by getting everything in your life to fall perfectly into place is as futile as jumping into a turbulent ocean and somehow hoping you will stay still.

The ancient scriptures of many religions have pointed out this dilemma for thousands of years: *All pain and suffering comes from attachment to that which is inevitably always changing.* When we spend our time and energy trying to get it all perfect on the outside, *we are focusing our attention in the wrong direction.*

So if what's outside is always changing, if your plates are always going to drop, if some of your expectations are always going to be disappointed, how can you create a sense of happiness and contentment in life? The answer is to go in the opposite direction from the one we're used to going in, *to make a shift from trying to create stability on the outside to creating it on the inside.*

This is the first secret about life I want to share with you:

SECRET NUMBER ONE:

EVERYTHING YOU NEED
TO BE HAPPY IS INSIDE OF YOU

What does this statement actually mean? It means that you already have the key to your own happiness inside of you. *It's your own inner state that determines whether or not you're happy, and not what happens to you on the outside. Maybe you didn't realize that, but it's true.* And you're already experiencing this amazing phenomenon every day.

Think back to a time in your life when you were doing something that "should" have made you happy, such as going out to eat at a wonderful restaurant, or attending a concert you'd been waiting to see, or traveling to an exciting vacation spot you'd looked forward to visiting, BUT . . . you couldn't enjoy what you were doing on the outside because you were feeling terrible *on the inside.* Maybe you were sitting all dressed up at the fabulous restaurant, but knew that someone you loved, such as one of your children or a family member, was ill, so you just couldn't enjoy the food or the atmosphere. Maybe you were in the audience at the concert you'd been waiting months to attend, but you just had a terrible day at work and were so angry about a situation there that you couldn't get excited about the show at all. Or maybe you were on an exotic vacation with your partner in one of the most beautiful places in the world, but he was being very cold, distant, and unromantic with you, and you felt so hurt that it didn't matter where you were.

What was making you unhappy in these situations? The restaurant? The concert? Being on vacation? No . . . in fact, these are the very things you thought *would* make you happy.

You know just how this works. It always starts with a simple desire: *"If I could just take a few weeks and go to Hawaii, I'd be so happy,"* you tell yourself. And you finally decide to do it. And you announce to all your friends that you are going, and you can't wait. And you think about it for months. *"Only three more weeks, and we'll be in Hawaii!" "Only one more week, and I'll be lying on the beach drinking a piña colada!"* Then finally you're there, and your husband isn't paying much attention to you, and you're feeling unloved, and you're lying on the beach feeling absolutely miserable. And suddenly, the same things that were supposed to make you happy are driving you crazy: it's too hot and the couple in the adjacent lounge chair is bugging you and you can't stand the hotel and you're having a crummy time and wish you'd never come in the first place.

Why isn't Hawaii making you happy when you were so sure it would? *Because Hawaii doesn't have the power to make you happy.* If it did, you'd be lying there thinking, *"To hell with the fact that my husband is acting like a slug—I'm in Hawaii!! Who cares if my marriage is on the rocks? Look at those gorgeous palm trees!! Gosh, I'm happy!"*

Hasn't this happened to you? Haven't you finally gone somewhere or done something you thought would make you feel wonderful, only it doesn't, and you wonder to yourself, "Gee, I paid a lot of money for this. I *should* be enjoying it. I *should* be having a good time. What's wrong?"

What's wrong is that nothing on the outside is ever going to be more powerful than your own inner state of consciousness. You could be in the most beautiful spot on the planet, but if your heart is hurting, or your mind is anxious, you'll be miserable. And the opposite is true as well—you could be in the most unappealing place, but if your inner state is joyous and contented, you will feel happy where you are. You will create your own paradise.

Living Life from the Inside Out

This is an amazing and radical revelation about one of the secrets of life:

Life happens from the inside out.
If you are happy,
it is because of what is going on inside of you.
If you are sad,
it is because of what is going on inside of you.
Your world is all happening inside of you.

The world itself is a neutral place. Nothing that happens to you is inherently positive or negative. It is your *interpretation* of it that makes it a positive or negative experience. *It is what you do with it inside yourself that makes it positive or negative.* In fact, nothing really happens to your true self on the outside. All of your reactions to life take place on the inside. That's why, whether you have understood it this way or not, *you are already living life from the inside out.*

Here are some examples of this principle:

Let's say you are in a relationship with a man. He comes to you one day and announces, "I don't want to be with you anymore. I am leaving." Is his leaving you a positive or negative event? The answer is: It is neither. His leaving is *neutral*. It is just an action. He is walking out. What is positive or negative is how you *react inside* to his leaving. If you are madly in love with him and think you are meant to be together, you will react with sorrow and conclude that his leaving is negative. If you were tired of him anyway, and trying to figure out a way to break it off yourself, you will react with relief, and conclude that his leaving is positive. Do you see how the same event can be experienced as producing happiness or sadness *when in fact, the event isn't doing anything—it's your inner state that is producing those emotions, those reactions?*

Here's another example: You are in a car accident and are seriously injured. You end up having to take a month off from work to stay at home and recover, and your mother, with whom you don't get along very well, comes to stay and take care of you. "This one is definitely *not* neutral!" you may be thinking. But look more closely. If you focus on how awful it is that you had the accident, that you are missing work, and that you have to put up with your mother, you will be unhappy and conclude that the accident was a negative event. But what if you take that time to contemplate your life and how fast you've been moving, and see that this month was a "forced vacation," so to speak, in which some higher power is insisting you slow down? And what if you realize that your mother is again able to feel useful in caring for you, in a way she hasn't for years, and that you are able to receive her love in this form, which is a great gift to her? And what if you allow yourself to feel vulnerable and out of control for the first time in a long while, and notice the harshness of your hard-driving personality softening in a way that is undeniably healthy? Then, in spite of your injury, you might feel a deep sense of well-being, and conclude that the accident was a very positive and, indeed, even necessary event.

Happiness is a decision you make to experience a situation in a particular way. It is not something that is bestowed upon you from the outside. It comes from the

inside out. In the same way, unhappiness isn't something that is inflicted upon you from the outside— it, too, is a choice you make.

You are the person with the most power to affect
your life.
You are the one who decides to be happy or unhappy
about what you are experiencing.

Isn't this a mind-bending discovery? Isn't this great news? The happiness you have been looking for is available at any time! It is right here, right now. You have been waiting for something on the outside to trigger your happiness, so you could give yourself permission to experience it, but the ability to be happy has been inside you all along. *In fact, happiness can only be attained from within.*

Nothing can make you happy without
your permission.
Nothing can make you unhappy without
your permission.

This is the meaning of Secret Number One: Everything You Need to Be Happy Is Inside of You—that you *already* possess the power to decide to be happy or unhappy. In this way, you create your own heaven or your own hell, your own contentment or your own misery, from moment to moment.

Understanding this principle is the first step in becoming emotionally and spiritually free, because you begin to see that *what you feel and experience at any time is ultimately up to you.* This kind of freedom isn't something anyone else can give you—it's the freedom only *you* can bestow on yourself by living each day from the inside out. Then you start to have true control over your life and your destiny, not by trying to make everything perfect on the outside, but by learning how to tap into your own source of happiness and peace on the inside.

Who Robs You of Your Ecstasy?

One of the reasons I made a serious commitment to my spiritual growth when I was still a teenager was that I was fed up with watching my state of well-being go up and down, up and down, depending upon what was happening in my life. No wonder I was so miserable—I felt like a boat without an anchor, or even a rudder, being tossed around by the stormy seas of circumstance. By the time I turned eighteen, I began formally practicing meditation, and I have continued this and other spiritual disciplines for the past thirty years. And at a certain point after I reached the age of forty-five, I thought I'd achieved a pretty steady state of consciousness. I was spending each summer on a spiritual retreat, where I would dive deep into my own inner silence and experience great tranquillity and contentment.

It was following a summer like this several years ago when suddenly, out of the blue, my life was bombarded by one painful challenge after another, professionally, personally, financially, you name it. It all seemed to hit me at once, like a cosmic hurricane, and no area of my world was left untouched. I remember waking up each morning, my stomach in knots, my heart hurting, not wanting to get out of bed, and thinking, *"What happened? Everything was going so well. Where did my peace of mind go?"*

In this state of emotional panic, I called someone very dear to me who is a female monk and meditation teacher. Tears fell from my eyes as I listed all of my personal dramas, tragedies, and dilemmas, each one sounding worse than the one before. She patiently and silently listened on the other end of the phone, and when I was finished, there was a long pause in the conversation. Then, in a very gentle but strong voice she said, "Barbara, who is robbing you of your ecstasy?"

"Finally," I thought to myself, "someone who understands what a terrible time I am going through!" and I began reciting names as an answer to her question: "This person is doing this to me, and this business associate did this to me, and this situation is doing this to me. . . ."

Again, and more firmly, she asked: "But Barbara, *who* is robbing you of your ecstasy?"

Suddenly, I felt as if someone had just thrown a bucket of cold water on my face and woken me up from a deep sleep. "Who is robbing you of your ecstasy?" All at once, I realized the profound truth that lay hidden in what she was asking. I *did* know how to contact my own happiness, my own ecstasy. Just a few months before, this woman had seen me in such a high, peaceful state, a state based on my own inner joy. Then I'd returned home to a turbulent time in my life, and *had allowed people and circumstances to rob me of that experience.* In fact, no one was really doing anything to me—I was doing it to myself by deciding that I couldn't be happy anymore if I had these problems or these situations. I was the cause of my own pain. I was robbing myself of my own ecstasy.

That phone call had a profound impact on me. In the days and weeks that followed, I looked carefully at my life "story," and realized that I had been allowing others to rob me of my ecstasy and personal happiness for as long as I could remember. Even though I had never been the victim type who actively and angrily blamed people or situations for my suffering, I did secretly feel that others were the cause of my pain. *"If you hadn't broken up with me, I would still be happy . . . if you hadn't tried to cheat me in business, I would still be happy . . . if this hadn't happened to me, I would still be happy."*

Somehow, the words my wise friend had used created a huge shift in my awareness. I was stunned to realize how much power I had been giving others over me without their even knowing it! And that was the key—that *I* was the one giving away that power, I was the one giving away my own happiness.

> No one else ever robs you of your happiness,
> your ecstasy.
> You rob yourself by making your ecstasy
> dependent upon others.

Since that powerful conversation with my friend, I have incorporated her question as a part of my own inner process of contemplation. Whenever I notice myself feeling unhappy, I stop and ask: "Barbara, who is robbing you of your ecstasy right now?" Of course, I ultimately arrive at the same answer: "I am." And that begins to point me back in the right direction, and reminds me that everything I need to be happy is, indeed, inside of me.

This is what's so exciting about Secret Number One:

> **The only thing wrong with you**
> **is that you don't understand**
> **that there is nothing wrong with you,**
> **that there is nothing essential missing.**

Nothing is going to make you more perfect or more whole than you already are now. You could finally find the right partner or get the right job or lose the right amount of weight or make the right amount of money, but it still wouldn't add to your perfection. It still wouldn't improve the essence of your soul. Who you really are inside doesn't need any improvement—it just needs to be recognized and understood.

So what is this place inside of you that is the source of happiness, of contentment, of your own ecstasy? Every religious and spiritual tradition in the world refers to this Perfect Self within us, that which is beyond our personality, our actions, our thoughts, and feelings. The Bible calls it the Kingdom of Heaven. In Eastern traditions, it is called the *atman* or the Buddha Nature. It is the essential, unchanging core within you. It is your consciousness, the part that knows you exist, and identifies you as *you*, and not someone else. It is your goodness, it is your passion, it is your peace, it is your love.

You already are familiar with this part of yourself. You have moments when you experience it, when you're in touch with yourself in a deep and meaningful way. Perhaps you're watching a breathtaking sunset, or giving a hug to a friend or family member, or doing a simple task like arranging flowers in a vase or making a salad, when suddenly you feel a surge of love rise up in your heart, and you're overcome with a recognition of rightness about the moment, as if everything is as it should be, as if everything makes sense.

What is it that you are feeling in these magical moments? *Your own love. Your own self. Your own source of happiness.* It's already and always there inside of you. In fact, it *is* the real you, the you underneath all of your fears and patterns and emotional wounds and forgetfulness.

Secret Number One says that when you learn how to drink from your own well of quiet inner joy, you will begin to experience a self-reliance that you could never achieve through any outer accomplishment or circumstance. It's not that you don't enjoy what comes to you on the outside in the form of your relationships and your daily pleasures. But you are no longer dependent on these to make you happy. You are no longer a prisoner of circumstances. You know that, ultimately, you are your own source of fulfillment. And this is when you become really free as a human being.

You Can't Prevent the Flood
But You Can Learn to Build an Ark

I never cease to be amazed at the extent to which the forces of life will go to make sure we get the essential lessons we need to learn. In my case, the lessons I've been confronted with have always been somewhat dramatic, probably to insure that as someone who teaches others, I always practice what I preach. So I will share with you something that happened to me while I was writing this book.

One night about ten o'clock, I was sitting upstairs in my home office working on this very chapter about happiness. It was late, but I was behind on my deadline, and I needed to use every spare minute in the days to come to complete the book on time. Needless to say, I was feeling like I was under a lot of pressure.

For weeks, I'd been writing and rewriting my thoughts on this first secret about happiness. I was particularly excited about the idea that each of us has the choice to be unhappy or happy in a given moment. In fact, I was enjoying this concept so much that when I heard a strange noise coming from downstairs, I ignored it, and kept writing. As I tried to find examples that would help me explain this understanding to you, I was aware in some part of my brain that there seemed to be a sound of gushing water in the background of my consciousness, but I assumed it was raining out, or that the dishwasher was on.

An hour and a half passed, and it was time to take a break. "That's odd," I commented to myself as I got up and began walking down the stairs. "That sound is still going on." As I put my foot down from the last step onto the living room floor, I was shocked to discover that I was stepping into six inches of water! The whole downstairs of my house was flooded, and what had been a faint noise of water now sounded like the roar of Niagara Falls coming from the pantry off the kitchen. I waded through the cold water as fast as I could, and when I opened the door into the pantry, a huge waterfall that was cascading from the ceiling came crashing down on me, instantly drenching my body from head to toe.

"Oh my God," I thought. "My whole house is flooding!" My next thought was, "Oh no, this can't be happening now." You see, I had just decided to move, and had put my house up for sale. We had a big open house scheduled in two days. And here I was in the middle of a flood.

I waded back into the kitchen, called 911, which connected me with the fire department, and then ran around assessing the situation. I could hardly believe my eyes. Half a foot of water covered everything—the bottom of the furniture, the carpets, anything that was on the floor. A strong current of water continued to pour from the pantry through the kitchen, into the living room, and all the way down the hall, carrying all kinds of items with it. I just shook my head in shock and amazement as I saw my dogs' beds floating by like boats on a stream.

I got the dogs and cat safely into a dry room just in time to answer the door. Three long, red fire trucks had arrived, and there on my doorstep stood twelve tall, muscular firemen all dressed in their hats and coats and loaded down with ropes, hoses, axes, and special equipment of every sort. I could tell from the looks on their faces that they were just as amazed at my appearance as I was at theirs—I resembled a drowned rat. My hair was plastered down on my head, my clothes were soaked all the way through, and my glasses were so wet that I could barely see.

Within two minutes, the supervisor had located the source of the problem—a hose that connected the water supply to the washing machine had developed a tiny crack, and the hundreds of pounds of water pressure that ran through the pipes had burst through the small tear and obviously had been pouring through my house for the past hour and a half. "You're lucky you were home," he shouted over the loud roar. "A few more hours, and your whole house could have been ruined, or you could have had an electrical fire." He turned off the valve and the water mercifully stopped.

Suddenly, everything was quiet, except for the sloshing sounds of the firemen walking through the rooms to determine how many pumps they would need to remove the water from my house. And then, I noticed something that completely amazed me: I was totally calm. In fact, I had been totally calm the whole time. Concerned, yes.

Worried, definitely. But when I checked, I could still feel this sense of well-being and warmth inside of me.

"This is weird," I remember thinking. "I should be really upset about this! My house is flooded. I'm standing here soaking wet in the middle of the night with firemen pumping gallons of water from my home. There is going to be major damage to my possessions and the structure. I am going to have to spend all kinds of time and money repairing it. The house sale will be delayed. I'll have to take time from my writing to do all this, and my book won't be finished in time."

The longer I thought about what was happening, the more suspicious I got about my state of mind. Maybe I was in shock. Maybe the severity of the situation just hadn't sunk in yet. But in the hours that followed, I became aware of something even more strange than my lack of unhappiness about the flood—I was actually enjoying myself! The firemen were all very nice and helpful, and I kidded them about how sweet it was of them to come up in the middle of the night to clean all my floors. They had recognized me from television, and teased me about how glamorous I looked soaking wet with a mop in my hand. The guys went about their business of trying to get the water out of my house with vacuums and special hoses, and I went about my business of picking up all the things that lay soaking on the floor. Somehow, I was having a good time.

I'd noticed one particular fireman grinning at me whenever I went by, and at one point, I walked past him with my arms full of dripping wet towels. He glanced up from his equipment and with a mischievous look on his face, said, "So Barbara: Are you having a 'real moment'?"

My book *Real Moments*® had been about learning how to make each experience in life meaningful. This guy had obviously read the book, and figured that I probably wasn't having an enjoyable "real moment" right then, and decided to tease me about it.

"You know," I answered with a smile, "I actually AM having a real moment right now!" And I was. Somehow, I was happy. Certainly, I was not pleased with the flood or the mess or the impending cleanup. *But on the inside, I still felt a state of contentment and peace that this incident had not been able to steal from me. I was grateful that I had been home. I was grateful that the firemen came so quickly. I was grateful that nothing worse had happened.*

It was long past midnight when the firemen had most of the water out of the house and had packed up to leave. By this time, we were all good buddies. On a whim, I ran upstairs to get my camera, and there in the middle of my wet living room we all posed for pictures together. They probably thought I was crazy, but I didn't care. I was having fun! And that was my thought as I waved good-bye to them and watched their big trucks drive away: *"This was fun!"*

When I went upstairs to turn off my computer, I looked at the screen and read the last thing I'd written before I'd gone downstairs and discovered the flood:

Nothing can make you happy without
your permission.

**Nothing can make you unhappy without
your permission.**

Standing there in my damp clothes, I knew that what I'd written was true. *I had not allowed the flood to make me unhappy.* It was just a series of neutral events, events that I easily could have used to make myself miserable but didn't. In fact, I'd found moments of joy, connection, and gratitude in the experience. I'd practiced the very principle I was writing about, and it had worked. The universe had actually given me a great gift that evening, one I would never forget.

That night as I lay in bed, I suddenly remembered a line I'd included in my proposal to the publisher for this book: "You can't stop the flood, but you can learn to build an ark."

Little did I know back then how prophetic these words were going to be. The flood had, indeed, come. And the ark of my own inner state of happiness had remained intact.

I fell asleep with a smile on my face.

*The foolish person seeks happiness in the distance;
the wise person grows it under his feet.*
JAMES OPPENHEIM

I began this chapter with a story about how God hid the secret for happiness in the human heart. So let me end with another story, this one about how God helped one woman find that very same secret in her own heart, but only when she was ready to stop looking for it on the outside.

The Greatest Wish of All

Once upon a time in a very small village in India, there lived a poor but pious woman who worshipped Lord Vishnu, the form of God that is responsible for maintaining all of creation. Each morning, before she did anything else, this dedicated woman would perform a *puja,* or ceremony, to the statue of him that she had in her house. She would offer flowers and fruits and incense before his form, and then bathe and dress the statue, chanting special hymns of love and gratitude. As she loved the Lord in this symbolic way, the woman's heart would swell with joy and wonder.

One day, Vishnu, moved by this woman's devotion, decided to appear before her. The woman was overcome with ecstasy at the miracle of seeing her beloved Lord, and tears of joy poured down her cheeks.

"You have pleased me with your diligent worship," the Lord said to his devotee. "I have decided to reward you. Ask me to fulfill any wish you desire."

The woman could hardly believe what she was hearing. What amazing good fortune! The Lord was offering her anything she wanted! Her mind began to race: *"What should I ask for? Riches? Many healthy children? A large and luxurious home? What about lasting beauty?"* She was so busy trying to decide what she wanted the most that she almost forgot about Vishnu standing right there in front of her.

"Please, Lord," she implored in a trembling voice, "May I have some more time to think this over? I just can't seem to make up my mind."

"Take as much time as you like," Vishnu replied compassionately, and with a parting smile, vanished.

The woman was beside herself with confusion. What should she do? How could she make such an important choice as this? She decided to ask her friends for their advice on what she should wish for, feeling that perhaps they would be more clear-minded about this than she was.

The next day, she called all of her friends together, and posed the question to them: What should her one wish be?

"Ask for money," the first friend insisted. "If you have money, you can buy whatever else you want."

"No, don't ask for money," the second friend disagreed. "What good is wealth if you don't have your health? You won't be able to enjoy the money. I tell you, you should ask for good health."

"Health isn't specific enough," a third friend advised strongly. "Ask for a long life, not just a healthy one, and give the Lord a specific number of years."

The devoted woman's husband, who was not very devoted himself and lacked good understanding of spiritual matters, had been standing there listening to these suggestions. "All your friends are fools," he declared in an irritated voice. "If this lord said you could ask for any boon you wanted, what about asking him for the boon of even more boons?"

All this time, the woman listened anxiously to everything her friends and her husband had to say, but still, none of their answers satisfied her.

Weeks and then months passed, and all the woman could think about was what to ask Vishnu. This dilemma consumed her awareness so completely that, without realizing it, she stopped worshipping the Lord in her morning ritual as she had done for her whole life. She stopped thinking about how much she loved him. She stopped chanting songs of praise to him. Instead, her mind was totally focused on what she wanted the Lord to give her. Soon, she began to lose all the joy she had possessed in her heart, and even her love for Vishnu began to evaporate.

Finally, a day came when the woman felt the last shred of inner contentment vanish from her soul. In a panic, she fell down on her knees and prayed fervently: "Oh, Lord Vishnu! Help me! You promised that you would grant me a great boon, and asked me what wish I wanted you to fulfill. But I cannot answer your question myself, and I can think about nothing else. Please, I beg you, tell me what to ask for!"

Before the woman could even finish her prayer, Lord Vishnu was manifested before her in all his splendor. "I thought you would never ask," he said, smiling. "Here is the boon you should request from me: **Ask to be happy in life no matter what you get.**"

The woman bowed her head, realizing the great wisdom in Lord Vishnu's teaching. And then she did as he said: she asked for and received that gift. And she lived out each and every day of her life on this earth with great serenity and joy, for no matter what she ever got or didn't get, she was always happy.

This is my highest wish for you—that like the woman in our story, you remember the source of happiness is always already inside you, offering you all you need to experience true joy in this and every moment.

The Purpose of Life Is for You to Grow into the Best Human Being You Can Be

*My favorite place to go
is where I've never been before.*

ANONYMOUS

When I was nine years old, I fell in love with a doll I saw advertised on television. The TV said the doll cried real tears and even wet her diapers—it was appropriately named a Betsy-Wetsy Doll—and I was determined to have it. After much hinting on my part, my mother agreed to buy the doll for me, and so one Saturday morning we set off for the neighborhood toy store. I shook with excitement as I entered the shop and saw that it was overflowing with trains, Tinkertoys, teddy bears, every imaginable object of a child's fantasy. I was sure I had arrived in heaven!

It didn't take long for me to spot Betsy-Wetsy waiting for me on the shelf. I scooped her lovingly into my arms, promising to change her diapers as often as needed. As I walked down the aisle toward the cash register, a display of brightly colored boxes suddenly caught my eye. I stopped and gazed in wonder at the title on one of the boxes: ENCHANTED CASTLE—A PLACE WHERE ALL YOUR DREAMS CAN COME TRUE! it read in glowing gold and purple letters. Beneath the headline was a picture of the most magical castle I had ever seen. The castle looked like it was made of silver; it seemed to rise several stories from the ground, and was covered with towers and turrets and moats. There were tiny windows everywhere, and my imagination went wild: I pictured a starry-eyed princess who lived in luxury peering out from those windows, longing for a glimpse of her Prince Charming, who, naturally, was racing toward the castle on horseback to carry her off to a land where they would live happily ever after. I stood there transfixed, sure that destiny had brought me into the toy store so that I, too, could make all of my dreams come true. I had to have that castle.

My poor mother didn't have a chance. I begged, I pleaded, I used every persuasive power that a seven year old has (which, in my case, was a considerable amount), and finally, she gave in. I walked out of the store with Betsy-Wetsy under one arm, and my Enchanted Castle under the other.

The car ride home was a blur. All I remember is racing up to my bedroom with my treasures, carefully taking them out of the paper bag, and placing them on my bed. I held Betsy in my arms for a minute before laying her down off to the side. After all, Betsy was just a doll, but in that box was an Enchanted Castle, and even at seven, I knew to choose magic over real life any day. Besides, I knew Betsy would understand. I carefully unwrapped the plastic covering from the large box, and opened the cardboard flaps. Slowly, with trembling hands, I reached into the depths of the box to lift my castle out of the darkness.

The Pieces of My Dreams

There was nothing there! I couldn't feel a thing in the box. No towers jutting up, no flags flying on the roof.

In fact, there was no roof at all! My heart pounded as my little hands reached deeper, and deeper, until finally, at the very bottom of the box, I could feel a pile of tiny objects. I spilled out the contents of the box and there before me, littering the top of my lace bedspread, lay the two hundred and seventy-seven pieces of the Enchanted Castle, ready for assembly, along with several tubes of model glue, paint, brushes, and a twenty-four-page instruction booklet.

I sank to the floor and stared in shock at the confusing mess on my bed. I felt completely crushed. I had expected a beautiful, magical castle, and instead I'd gotten a pile of plastic parts. Now my dreams would never come true. I began to sob the deep, hopeless sobs of someone who has decided the world is a cruel and unfair place.

Just then, my mother knocked on my bedroom door, and when she heard me crying, she rushed in and took me in her arms. "What's wrong, sweetheart?" she asked with a concerned look on her face. "Aren't you happy with your presents?"

"It's, it's the cc . . . cc . . . castle," I stammered. "It's not right."

"What's not right about it?" my mother questioned. "Here, let me take a look." She got up and stood over the bed. "Let's see, they included glue, five colors of paint, good . . . brushes, and here's the instructions. Honey, everything looks O.K. to me."

I listened to her in bewilderment. How could she say

the castle looked O.K.? "But Mommy," I sniffed, "the castle is all in little pieces. It's not pretty and fixed like the picture on the box."

My mother pulled me toward her and took my hands in hers. "Barbara," she said softly, "There's nothing wrong with the castle. It is supposed to come in pieces like that—that's the whole idea. It's a model and you are supposed to put it together. See, honey, here's the instructions, they show you how to stick the pieces that fit onto one another. And then you put a little glue on them so they will stay that way, and when it is all glued together, you paint it with these paints, and you're all finished, and the castle will look just like the one on the cover."

"But I thought it was supposed to come *already* made!" I shook my head in disbelief. "You mean I have to put the whole castle together myself? That ruins the whole thing—it will never be as good as the one in the picture. And besides, because I'll know *I* put it together, it won't be magical at all!" And then I burst into more tears.

Putting the Castle Together

I don't remember how long I ignored my castle. I know that I put it back in the box that night and left it on a shelf in my closet. I was furious that it hadn't come already made, that I was expected to do something to make it work. I decided that Betsy-Wetsy was the one for me after all, and spent my time pouring water into Betsy's mouth and waiting for it to come out the other end so I could change her diapers. I soon grew tired of cleaning her up—after all, how many times can you change a rubber baby before the thrill is gone? So one afternoon, I found myself taking the Enchanted Castle out of the closet and placing it on the bed. I opened the instruction booklet and began to read.

It took me several weeks to build my castle. At first, I was very frightened. *"What if I make a mistake?"* I thought to myself, *"and glue the wrong pieces together? What if I can't figure out what goes where? What will I do if I can't understand the directions?"* It wasn't long before I found out the answers: I did make mistakes, and had to unglue dozens of little plastic pieces and reglue them in the right place. I did get confused at certain points, and had to ask my mother to help me out. But as the days passed, and I could see the beginnings of a castle forming before my eyes, my fear turned into excitement, the frustration turned into challenge. I would race home from school so I could work on the castle. I would secretly stay up way past my bedtime gluing and assembling, and when it was almost finished, painting.

And then one day, it was done. I sat on my bed and stared at my Enchanted Castle in its place of honor by the window. I knew that it didn't look exactly like the castle in the picture—the paint was smeared in a few places, the glue hadn't always dried evenly. But it looked beautiful, and it looked magical. And even more miraculously, I felt magical: I was completely happy and fulfilled, not just because I had an Enchanted Castle to play with, but because I had helped to create that castle. And the castle meant much more to me this way than if it had come ready made, perfect, leaving nothing for me to do but admire it. For the real magic of the castle was that even though it looked like I was putting it together, it was putting me together.

It has been almost thirty years since I made that trip to the toy store. In the decades that have passed, I've faced many challenges, trials, and crises, both personally and professionally. There were times when my life looked nothing like the picture I'd always had of how things would turn out for me, but instead, resembled a confused pile of little pieces similar to that castle spread on top on my bed. And at these moments, I often felt angry, frustrated, and frightened, just like I had when I was seven: *"Why do things have to be this way?"* I'd cry. *"Why does life have to be so hard?"*

But each time I'd experience these feelings, I'd remember my castle. For just as the ad on the box had promised, my Enchanted Castle did help me learn how to make my dreams come true, my highest dreams: It taught me that life was about putting myself together, and not coming already "finished." It taught me that the purpose of my life wasn't to make everything look perfect on the outside, but to grow on the inside as the events of my destiny worked to teach me patience, courage, and self-acceptance.

What Is the Purpose of Your Life?

I share this story with you because it illustrates one of the most important points of this book—*that when we don't understand how something is supposed to work, if we aren't clear about its purpose, we can incorrectly conclude that there is a problem where there isn't one at all.* When I was nine, I thought the purpose of getting that castle was to take it out of the box ready made and enjoy it. I didn't understand that its real purpose was to teach me certain skills and lessons, and ultimately, to give me a sense of self-confidence I never would have attained if I hadn't been forced to put those pieces together. This same principle applies to every part of our lives—if we don't understand the purpose of what we're going through, then we can misjudge the experience and even the outcome.

So what is the purpose of your life? Have you ever asked yourself that challenging question? What is the purpose of each year? Of each day? And how do you know whether or not you have fulfilled that purpose when you go to sleep each night, or on New Year's Eve each year as you evaluate the twelve months past, or at the end of your life as you look back over how you have lived? How do you know whether or not your life has been successful?

Each of us has our own answers. Maybe you feel one of the purposes of your life is to get married and raise a family, or to create a comfortable lifestyle and a beautiful home, or to have a stimulating and rewarding career, or perhaps something less personal and more global, such as to contribute something valuable and lasting to society. And there are subpurposes and goals, as well—for instance, that you want to travel, or to make sure all of your children graduate from college, or to build up your business so you can leave a large inheritance to your grandchildren.

These purposes become what I call your "shoulds":

I should be happily married by a certain age.
I should have children and they should turn
    out a certain way.
I should have the home I've always dreamed of.
I should have a rewarding career.
I should do something with my artistic talents.
I should be making a certain amount of money.
I should be helping others.
I should weigh a certain amount, and no more.
I should be more successful than my parents were.
I should have a certain amount of money saved
    up for my retirement.
I should have done certain things and gone to
    certain places before I die.

Now, imagine that a friend you haven't spoken to for a while calls you up one day and asks, "How have you been doing?" What determines your answer? How do you decide how you have been doing? You probably do the same thing that I and everyone else does—you unconsciously check your list of "shoulds" and see how many of them you are able to check off as "done," and how many are still incomplete. Or to use the analogy from my introduction, you check your plates to see which ones are spinning and which have fallen. Your "shoulds" become the basis upon which you evaluate how successfully you have been living.

Let's say that in the past month, you went through a painful breakup with a man you'd been in love with, your company downsized and informed you that you should start looking for a new job, you were overdrawn on two credit cards, and you gained five pounds. How would you most likely respond when your friend asks, "How are you doing?" You know the answer: "I'm not doing well at all. In fact, I'm having a terrible month!" Perhaps you're feeling like a failure; perhaps your self-esteem has plummeted. Perhaps your faith in life itself has been shaken, because nothing is turning out the way you think it should.

If you believe that the purpose of your life that month is to be in a great relationship, or have a stable job, or pay off your credit cards, or maintain the perfect weight, you will, indeed, feel like a failure. You will berate yourself and conclude that you are having a "bad" month, that somehow, you are blowing it. You will make yourself suffer.

This is how you sabotage your sense of self-esteem. You evaluate yourself based on a set of misunderstandings about what the purpose of your life really is. But the truth is, nothing that most of us have on our "should" list is the purpose of life.

Here is the second of our ten secrets:

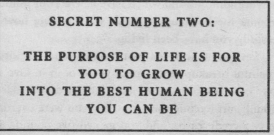

SECRET NUMBER TWO:

**THE PURPOSE OF LIFE IS FOR
YOU TO GROW
INTO THE BEST HUMAN BEING
YOU CAN BE**

What this secret *doesn't* say is as important as what it *does* say. It *doesn't* say that the purpose of life is to find the right partner, or become successful, or to raise a family, or to contribute something valuable to the planet, or even to feel good. It says that the purpose of your life is for you to grow.

This is one of the most basic metaphysical truths there is. This secret says, in effect, *that life on earth is a classroom, and that you and I and everyone are students, here to learn certain lessons.* In other words, life is not supposed to just go smoothly. Things are not supposed to be perfect. We are supposed to experience challenges. We are supposed to undergo difficulty. We are here to learn.

The problem is that we have forgotten this great truth, this purpose of our lives. It's as if we sign up to come to earth thinking it is going to be some fabulous vacation spot. Then we are born, we arrive here, and begin to discover that things aren't the way we thought they'd be. We encounter difficulty, we encounter pain, we encounter obstacles, and we become confused and disoriented. Surely there has been some mistake! The brochure said it was a paradise. So why are we being forced to go through all of these hardships?

Many of us never recover from the shock of discovering that life on earth is more like a classroom than Club Med. "You mean I'm supposed to work on myself, to go through a series of often painful lessons? This is NOT what I had in mind at all! I thought this was supposed to be about pleasure, about comfort, about fun. I don't want to be in school! I am ready for recess!"

Doesn't this sound an awful lot like the nine-year-old Barbara having a tantrum when she discovered that her magic castle didn't come all perfectly put together, but rather, required patient and careful assembly? Now, imagine that my mother hadn't explained to me that nothing was wrong with my castle, that it was *supposed* to be in pieces, that I was *supposed* to go through the process of putting it together. If I hadn't known this, I might have erroneously concluded that I had somehow ruined the castle before I got it home, or that something was wrong with what I'd been given, or that the store had ripped me off.

Most people are born with an unconscious expectation that they are supposed to come into this world already put together, already very competent at living and loving. There comes a point in each of our lives when we have the unpleasant experience of realizing that we didn't come all put together, and that, in fact, we are still in pieces. We look at our lives, and they do not resemble the pictures we have in our heads of how things should be turning out. And we conclude that something must be wrong with us, that we are failing at life. And we stop loving ourselves.

There is nothing wrong with you. You've simply forgotten what you signed up for when you came here. Life isn't supposed to be easy. It isn't supposed to be a smooth ride. It is designed to be challenging so that you will grow into a more conscious, loving human being.

If you look around you at the physical universe, you will see that its nature is growth. Everything from the cells in your body to the planets orbiting the sun are constantly growing, constantly changing, constantly evolving. Nothing stays still. Nothing remains the same. So think about it—why would your life be the exception? Why would you be the only thing that exists in all of creation whose purpose *isn't* to grow?

I once heard a thought-provoking quote: *A diamond is a piece of coal that stuck to the job.* Imagine this tiny piece of coal buried deep in the earth. If you had no understanding of the miraculous ways of Nature, you might examine the black rock and conclude that it was inert, and that it couldn't possibly "grow." But if you came back thousands of years later to unearth that same rock, you'd be astonished to discover that it had transformed itself into a magnificent and valuable diamond.

It stuck to the job, to its purpose, which was to grow and become the most beautiful gem it could.

We are all pieces of rock becoming diamonds. And just as the earth which encases that piece of coal puts pressure on it, heats it, and exposes it to the necessary conditions that will enable it to turn into a sparkling diamond, so life is putting pressure on us, challenging us, exposing us to whatever it is we need to grow into the most loving and wise human beings we can be.

How to Make Every Day of Your Life a Great Day

The powerful understanding contained in Secret Number Two can radically change your experience of life in every moment. Rather than judging yourself and your life based on how perfectly you are fitting into a picture of how you think things "should" be, you begin to evaluate yourself and your life based on how much you are growing, how much you are learning. This is the magic formula for making every day of your life a great day.

When you think the purpose of life
is to do or get or accomplish,
you will always feel like a failure
when things don't turn out as planned.
When you understand that life is a classroom

in which success means growing into
the best human being possible,
you begin evaluating yourself and your experiences
from a totally different point of view.

Each day of your life, you consciously or unconsciously evaluate yourself—how did I do today? For instance, suppose you work in sales for a living, and you have a week where you encounter one difficult customer after another, the result being that you close no sales and make no commissions. At the end of that week you would probably think, "What a lousy week! I didn't close one deal. I am so disappointed in myself. What is wrong with me?"

If you're evaluating yourself based on the premise that the purpose of your life is to close deals, or to make money, or to achieve certain material goals, then yes, you had a lousy week. But what if you decided to evaluate yourself based on the premise that the purpose of your life is to grow? Maybe during that week, in spite of how obnoxious those potential customers were, you maintained a cheerful and kind attitude. Maybe during that week, in spite of how disheartened you felt, you didn't give up, resort to stuffing your face with junk food, or getting down on yourself. Maybe you exhibited patience, you were compassionate with people, you kept going, you didn't lose your temper with anybody, you didn't go off your diet, you didn't do anything unhealthy to cover up what you were feeling.

So now how does the week look to you? It was a

fabulous week, a triumphant week! You truly fulfilled your purpose that week by learning, meeting your challenges with steadiness and perseverance. You may not have achieved the material rewards you wanted, but you achieved something far more profound and lasting—*you grew into a better human being.*

Have you been feeling bad about yourself lately? Do you look at your life and conclude that you aren't doing as well as you think you should? Perhaps you haven't been looking at your life from the correct point of view. Perhaps you are missing your own great achievements because you're judging yourself by standards that don't even apply to you anymore. Secret Number Two suggests that it is time to change your paradigm of what success means to you.

> Instead of defining your success
> by what you have achieved or acquired,
> why not begin defining your success
> by how much you are growing each day?

So how do you begin? *Take your "should" list and throw it away.* Then, replace it with just one commitment:

> "Today I want to grow into the best human being
> I can be."

Tell yourself, "I want to learn as much as I can and grow as much as I can with whatever comes my way." Then no matter what happens to you on the outside, it can be a great day, a successful day, based on how you are handling the day *on the inside*.

How Can You Have a Successful Day from the Inside Out?

If you learn even one new thing about yourself today, it will be a successful day.

If you handle one situation with another person a little better than you have before, it will be a successful day.

If you are more patient and compassionate with someone else or yourself, it will be a successful day.

If you gain a little bit more understanding about something or someone, it will be a successful day.

If you resist indulging in an old, unhealthy pattern of behavior or of thinking and instead choose a new one, it will be a successful day.

If you are kind to someone else, or to yourself, it will be a successful day.

If you love yourself even though you don't do everything perfectly, it will be a successful day.

> If you are grateful for the gift of being alive and
> for the opportunity to learn and grow, it will
> be a successful day.

This is such an uplifting way to approach your life. Instead of seeing existence as a series of tests that you pass or flunk each day, why not see it as an opportunity for growth, for learning? Then, instead of "bad days" or "good days," you end up with days in which perhaps you have grown more or grown less, but all of them are successful days.

Remembering this principle has made a huge difference in my own life. Being a perfectionist and an achievement-oriented person, I used to have such a long list of "shoulds" for myself each day that I made it virtually impossible for me to feel successful, to feel fulfilled. The result was that I was having too many "bad days," not because anything bad was happening, but because I was misunderstanding the purpose of my day, and therefore judging myself and the day incorrectly. Lately I have been consciously remembering Secret Number Two, and whenever I notice that I think I'm having a "bad day," or even a "bad hour," I stop and ask myself:

> "What am I learning today?"
> "How am I growing today?"

Instantly, I discover something that I wasn't seeing before, something I wasn't appreciating about myself or the challenges I am facing. I always come away from these moments of contemplation feeling more love for myself.

How to See Yourself Through God's Eyes

I like to think of this process as seeing your life through God's eyes, and not your eyes. (If you want, you can substitute the idea of Universal Intelligence or whatever image of a higher power feels comfortable to you, but the concept is the same.) God isn't sitting there thinking, "She didn't make one darn sale today. She's a failure in my book," or "She's ten pounds overweight again! She's just blowing her life," or "Oh no, another breakup with a boyfriend? What was I thinking when I created her?"

Do you really think if there is a cosmic force responsible for creating this universe that it would judge you on things as mundane as these? In fact, I don't believe we are being judged at all. I believe we are being encouraged and cheered on and watched over and picked up each time we fall.

> Learning to love yourself means
> beginning to see yourself through God's eyes.

Several years ago, I was going through a painful time in which I had to admit to myself that I had misjudged certain situations in my life and made what I considered to be some serious mistakes. The more I understood the choices I had made, the worse I felt about myself. "How could I have been so stupid?" I lamented. "I've been working on myself for so long. I should have paid more attention. How could I have missed what is now so obvious?"

It was in this mood of severe self-criticism that I decided to sit down and meditate, which is my daily practice. I closed my eyes, and for a while just watched the continual parade of negative thoughts about myself march through my mind. Then at some point, I slipped into a very deep state of meditation and entered a space of peace and stillness.

Suddenly, I felt myself transported into a world of brilliant blue light. All around me, I could feel the presence of the most loving beings I had ever encountered. I knew instinctively that these were angels, spiritual guides whose job was to watch over human beings during our time here on earth. These guides welcomed me with such delight and seemed overjoyed to see me. I could sense a divine sweetness emanating from their eyes, from their voices, as if the only emotion they were capable of was love.

Still deep in meditation, I became aware that tears of sadness were falling from my eyes as I silently confessed to these beautiful beings how disappointed I was in myself, and how much I felt I'd let them and God down by not being a better person and learning my lessons more quickly. I felt all the grief and anger I'd been carrying over the past weeks pour out of my heart. These beings listened and nodded with great compassion.

Then I heard a soft voice begin to speak to me, and I knew it was a voice that spoke for all of them. The message it transmitted to me didn't come in these exact words, for it contained much more than the words that I received. But I will share the essence of what I was given. It said:

"My child, we are in such awe of what you are doing on earth. We watch you in amazement and with great pride. How courageous you are! How persistent you are! How willing you are to grow, to experience, to feel! You are doing so well! You are not making mistakes. We do not see mistakes, only lessons learned, or lessons not yet learned. If all of you could only know for one second how beautiful you appear to us, how much we honor you for being willing to take on a human body and grow as souls, you would never judge yourselves again, you would never feel that you were failing. We love you. . . ."

As I received this message in my heart, I experienced waves of joy and happiness washing over me. In that moment, I KNEW that what I was hearing was true, that you and I and all of us *are* being watched over with such compassion and being loved so unconditionally, beyond anything we could ever imagine. For a brief moment, I saw a vision of the multitude of human beings on earth, each trying to find his way, to live out her chosen role in the cosmic drama. Everyone looked perfect to me, just as he or she was. Everyone was doing the best he or she could. Suddenly, I, too, felt that same unconditional love for humanity, and the tears streaming down my face this time were tears of joy. The last thing I remember hearing was that ethereal voice saying, "Now you know how we feel about you."

I wanted to share this experience with you, even though it is a very personal one, because it irrevocably changed the way I felt about myself and others. I have never forgotten that feeling of total acceptance, and I believe with all my heart that each and every one of us is being loved completely and unconditionally. I don't always find it easy to see myself with that same pure vision as those beings saw me, but even when I can't, I know they are still there on some plane of existence, peering down on me with great excitement and compassion, saying, "Ooooh, look what she's going through now! How brave she is! What an important lesson she has chosen to learn!"

You are not making mistakes.
We do not see mistakes, only lessons learned,
or lessons not yet learned.

This is such a beautiful and important message for us to remember! It eliminates the concept that when we make mistakes, we have somehow lost our goodness, that we have failed. A mistake is a lesson learned. And if we make the same mistake again, it is a lesson not quite learned, but one we can be sure we will be given the opportunity to learn over and over again until we get it right!

Often when I am interviewed by a reporter during a book tour, or on a television appearance, he or she will get around to the subject of my personal life. Invariably,

I get a question like, "Why do you feel qualified to teach others about love and relationships when you seem to have made so many mistakes yourself?" Whenever I am asked this, I use the moment as an opportunity to, shall we say, clear up the person's "misunderstanding" about the concept of mistakes.

"What mistakes?" I respond with a smile. "I haven't made mistakes. But I have learned A LOT of lessons! And I've grown from every single one of them. I guess since I'm growing so much, I must be doing really well!"

At the end of one such TV interview, a cameraman approached me as I was getting ready to leave the studio. "I loved what you told the host," he said with a grin. "And I want to share something with you that my grandmother always told me when I was growing up: 'Just because I make a mistake doesn't mean I AM a mistake!' "

"I love it!" I replied. "May I pass it on to others?"

He grinned even wider. "My grandma would be happy to know you did."

Isn't this a wonderful phrase to remember? *Just because I make a mistake doesn't mean I AM a mistake.* And we can take it one step further and remind ourselves that what we think is a mistake is just a lesson in disguise, waiting to be learned.

If Growth Is So Good for Me, Why Does It Feel So Bad?

Even when we believe that all we've been discussing is true, that the purpose of life is to grow, that we are here to learn lessons, still, it's not always easy to love ourselves in the midst of a period of "growth." Why is this? *Because growth is usually not a comfortable experience.* It can be scary. It can be painful. One reason for this is that in order to grow, you need to change from who and what you were to something new. And change involves letting go. You can't grow without letting go of where you were.

Imagine you are holding really tightly onto something in your hand. Suddenly, you see something else that you want more than what you have. What do you do? You don't even think about it—you open your hand, and you pick up the new item. But in the process, what else have you done? You've let go of what was originally in your hand.

Growth always costs us something. We see this truth in Nature all the time. The bud of a rose starts out covered in tight leaves, but when the bud begins to grow and open, the green coverings get ripped to pieces. When a flower is ready to shoot forth from the ground, the dirt that was in that place gets thrown to the side as the shoot comes up.

**Moving forward in life always costs us the past.
Everything that we gain always costs us
what we must let go of.**

Letting go is never easy, and almost always makes us uncomfortable, as we will discuss in the next few chapters. *And because it makes us uncomfortable, we often erroneously conclude that something bad is happening to us when we are being forced to let go and to grow, because it doesn't feel good.*

This is such an important point to understand, and one of the most essential secrets about life:

> **There is a difference between**
> **what is pleasant and what is beneficial.**

Just because something is unpleasant, or makes you uncomfortable, doesn't mean it is not beneficial or not good for you. In fact, often it is what makes us most uncomfortable that serves us the most. If you go to the doctor and he says, "I am going to have to perform some procedures that will be painful, but they will be good for you," you wouldn't question him and respond, "How can they be good for me if they are unpleasant?" Your common sense tells you that in the science of medicine, many procedures that are beneficial in helping your body remain healthy or heal may, indeed, not be very pleasant. However, we often forget to translate this same understanding to other parts of our lives.

Have you ever gone through a very challenging, uncomfortable time that you can now look back on and say, "I grew so much—it was the best thing that ever happened to me"? At the time, it was the worst thing that had ever happened to you. Why? Because it didn't feel good. Because it made you so uncomfortable. It was impossible for you to imagine how something beneficial could be happening when you felt so miserable.

This is how we often mistake times of tremendous growth as "bad times": **We misinterpret the discomfort for something that isn't beneficial.** We conclude that we must be doing something wrong. How could something good be happening when everything looks like a mess? But actually, discomfort usually means that you are in the midst of great growth. And the opposite can be true, as well—when you are feeling really comfortable for long periods of time, it may be that you aren't growing much at all.

Secret Number Two says: **The purpose of life is for you to grow into the best human being you can be.** We need to remind ourselves of this principle again and again, so that we can recognize our growth, honor ourselves for our growth, and find the courage to keep growing. And we need to remind each other—our partners, our friends, our children—so that when we see them growing and learning lessons, we can say, "I'm so proud of you. You are so courageous. You're doing so well," rather than buying into the old illusions that because things don't look perfect, there must be something wrong.

· · ·

No matter how much I teach these principles to others, I still need those same reminders myself. Recently I was experiencing one of those "growth spurts," when many areas of my life suddenly decided to teach me lessons all at the same time. Even though I have spent the past few years lecturing on these ten secrets, my first reaction to my plates wobbling was, "Oh no! Not again!"

Fortunately, I know that when I feel like I'm not seeing things the way they really are, it's time for me to talk to one of my close friends so he or she can straighten me out. And so I called a friend of mine named Ron Scolastico, who is a great teacher, author, and a great channeler of wisdom.

"Ron," I began, "I can't believe my life is in a state of upheaval again. I thought I finally had everything under control, and that things would calm down for a while. But so much is changing, for the hundredth time! And I feel so unsettled and uncomfortable. What am I doing wrong?"

"Barbara," Ron said, "don't forget that when you came into this life, on the form you filled out about what you wanted, you didn't check the box next to *Stability*, you checked the box next to *Growth*."

Instantly, I started to laugh. Because I knew in my heart that what he was saying was true. That's what I wanted. I hadn't checked the stability box. I checked *Growth* and then I underlined it and put stars and arrows around it, and then handwrote a little note next to it that said: "Please, please, as much as growth as possible!" And then, of course, I forgot about the form and was born. And ever since I can remember, I sure have been growing!

You must have filled out one of those same forms and checked the same box that I did, or you wouldn't be reading this book. I'm glad we are growing together. Doesn't it feel good to know that you are living your purpose here on earth?

Change Is Inevitable, So Stop Resisting and Surrender to Life's Flow

You can't stop the waves,
but you can learn to surf.

ANONYMOUS

There is one underlying reality present everywhere in our physical universe: *change*. Day turns into night and night turns back into day; summer turns into autumn and then winter. The cells of your body are all changing at this very moment. In fact, there is nothing about the universe that isn't changing right now. **Change is inevitable, and therefore everything in life is impermanent, and constantly moving. Nothing stays the same for very long.**

Nature doesn't complain about the fact that it is expected to constantly go through changes. For instance, can you imagine Nature saying, "You know what, I'm getting awfully tired of having to go through these seasons every year—it's exhausting. I think this year I'll skip winter and spring and autumn, and just stay in summer for a while," or "I'm so dizzy from these planets always revolving, round and round. I need a rest! I think I'll stop spinning just for a week or two." No, life flows on in an ever-changing succession of miraculous transformations.

We human beings, on the other hand, have a different attitude toward change: we're not always crazy about it. In fact, often we do everything we can to resist change and stay where we are, no matter how much we're being pointed in a new direction.

Here's one of my favorite anecdotes about change:

Jimmy had four pet goldfish that his parents bought him for his ninth birthday. Every night before he went to bed, he would watch the delicate, orange-colored fish swim round and round the small glass bowl they lived in. One day, he noticed that the water in the bowl looked kind of cloudy, and the glass was covered with a light film. Jimmy's mom explained to him that this was natural—the goldfish bowl needed to be cleaned.

Jimmy knew how to clean the bowl. He'd seen his friend Howie do it. He filled up his bathtub with cool water, and then gently lowered the bowl into the tub, until the four goldfish swam out of the dirty bowl into the bath-water. Jimmy spent the next fifteen minutes scrubbing the glass bowl until it was sparkling clean. Finally, it was all ready.

As Jimmy knelt by the bathtub to retrieve his goldfish, he saw a strange sight: Even though the bathtub was over four feet long and three feet wide, the four goldfish were swimming round and round in a tiny circle, right where Jimmy had originally placed them.

"Mom," yelled Jimmy, "come and look at the goldfish." Jimmy's mom came into the bathroom to see what all the fuss was about.

"Why are the fish swimming in a little circle when they have a whole tub?" Jimmy asked.

Jimmy's mom smiled at her son and answered, "Because they don't know they are in the tub. They think they are still at home in their tiny glass bowl. That's what they are used to."

It's true, isn't it, that often you and I are not that different from Jimmy's goldfish—even when we're offered an opportunity to change, to grow, we may decide instead to remain the way we've been, living within our same little boundaries, swimming in our same little circles. We choose the familiar over the unfamiliar, the old over the new. We get attached to staying in our comfort zone and resist taking the risks and flowing with the changes that would force us to face the unknown. And sometimes even when life makes those changes for us, like those goldfish, we stubbornly try to hang on to our old realities and fight the transformation that is already taking place.

How do many of us deal with our resistance to change? We do whatever we can to create certainty, security, a sense of being in control. We try to get everything in our lives all lined up and predictable. It's as if we think: "O.K., first I'll find a good job, then I'll find the right partner, have kids, hopefully be able to buy a nice house, and then everything will be in place, and I'll try my best to keep it that way for the rest of my life until I die." Our years become defined by the predictability of routines to which we cling fiercely: "This is how we will celebrate the holidays, and this is where we will go on vacation, and this is what time we will eat dinner, and this is what fits in and what doesn't. And please—no surprises—I don't want any surprises. I want things to be nice and calm."

How many times have you heard someone use these phrases, or even used them yourself?

"I don't want to rock the boat."
"Everything's fine the way it is."
"Why do we have to stir things up?"
"This is the way we've always done things."

These statements are based on a philosophy that says life is about avoiding change at all costs. We tiptoe through life until we die, hoping not to disturb anything, or to look too closely at anything in case, God forbid, we might have to make a change.

Are You Clinging to Your Comfort Zone?

Do you sleep on the same side of the bed every night? I have a sneaking suspicion that you do! Well, imagine that tonight when it's time for you to go to sleep, you walk into your room and find your partner lying on "your" side of the bed. "Why are you on *my side?*" you ask indignantly. And if your partner tells you that he has decided from now on that he's taking that side for himself, you would probably become agitated and reply, "But that's *my* side! I can't sleep on the other side!"

Have you ever wondered why you sleep on the same side of the bed? Is there something wrong with the other side? No, it's just that the side of the bed you are used to is *your side,* your "comfort zone," and moving out of it, if only by two feet, would make you very *un*comfortable.

What exactly is a "comfort zone"? Simply put, *it is wherever or whatever you have been; it is what you are used to; it is the little circle inside the fish tank; it is home*—a combination of situations and circumstances you set up based on those "shoulds" we talked about in the last chapter. Your comfort zone contains everything that is *familiar* to you, from your daily routines to the people you're used to having around. It extends to your emotional habits as well, such as how open you're used to being in your intimate relationships, how honest you're willing to be with yourself and others, and things such as this.

You probably experience this strong attachment to your comfort zone in small ways every day: finding out someone has parked in your assigned parking space at work, and noticing that you feel annoyed having to park somewhere else; getting upset if someone rearranges the things on your desk differently from the way you're used to placing them; having certain seats on buses, in theaters, in meeting rooms that you consider "your" seat, and feeling disturbed when someone takes it from you; using the same Exercycle at the gym week after week and feeling very irritated when someone else is on it, and you're forced to use another one.

Of course, there's nothing wrong with creating situations in our lives in which we are comfortable, or with preferring one side of the bed, or liking the second Exercycle on the left. The problem is that we end up trying to hold on to our comfort zone even when change is inevitable, when we have no control over what is happening, and we resist the new directions in which we're being taken. Our reaction at these times is usually, *"Oh no, everything was going along so smoothly, why did this have to happen?"*

"We were getting along so well, why did you have to bring up this problem? See what you've done? We're fighting and now our evening is ruined."

"I liked the way we used to write up our sales reports. Why are they changing the procedure? I hate these new forms. What a headache!"

"Why did they rearrange the aisles in this supermarket? Before, I knew where everything was. Now I can't find anything."

"But we always take our vacation with my cousins at the lake. Why do you want to do something different? It's so much easier to just go where we're used to going."

"I've always been such a healthy person. I can't believe the doctor told me I have high blood pressure and have to change my diet. I've never had a problem before. Why is my body doing this to me?"

These comments reflect our attitude toward change: **When things change, we often react with discomfort, resistance, even anger.** And naturally, the more changes we're faced with, and the more significant those changes are, the more unhappy we tend to become. Why? Because we feel somehow we've failed to keep our lives under control. Somehow, we have "lost" the battle to maintain consistency and stability, and some other force outside of ourselves has "won."

How much energy do you spend trying to stay in your comfort zone, trying to protect yourself from or prevent change in your life? Probably more than you'd like to admit. What is the result? It's the same for all of us:

**When we try to keep things the same,
we often end up holding onto people and situations
we shouldn't,
and ignoring the possibilities for transformation
that are presented to us.**

We stop our growth, and thereby sabotage our own progress, our own happiness. We become rigid, inflexible, stubborn. And of course, then we wonder why we don't feel the passion we want to feel, why our relationships become boring, why life seems meaningless at times, never suspecting that it's because we are trying so hard to keep things static, to keep life from moving.

Here is our third principle about life:

SECRET NUMBER THREE:

**CHANGE IS INEVITABLE,
SO STOP RESISTING AND
SURRENDER TO LIFE'S FLOW**

Did you ever see one of those silly, science-fiction movies from the 1950s or 1960s where some creatures from outer space invade the earth? I seem to remember the proverbial scene where one of these so-called aliens, usually dressed in a costume that seemed to be made of aluminum foil, approaches the frightened residents of the small town in which the spaceship had landed, and, in a very nasal-sounding voice, announces:

"Resistance is futile!"

That's really the message of Secret Number Three: When we resist change, we resist life's natural movement toward more, life's natural tendency to expand, to unfold. When we resist change, we are in essence trying to make life stand still. And nothing could be more unnatural. It would be like trying to make a river stop flowing, or the ocean stop moving, or your body stop breathing. That's called death. Death is the only state in which nothing about you or your life will change. And trying to keep things smooth and unchanging is a choice in the direction of death, and not life.

Resistance is futile. Why? Because change is inevitable. It's going to happen to us whether we like it or not, and whether we cooperate with it or not. In fact, the more we try to resist it, the more we are going to create suffering for ourselves and others. Secret Number Three suggests that instead of trying so hard to keep everything the way it has always been, we should stop struggling against the flow of life and learn to surrender to its currents.

**Life isn't about getting everything in place
and keeping it that way.**

> **That isn't called living—it's called stagnation,
> it's called death.
> Trying to get our lives to be "stable" and not rock the
> boat
> is the perfect formula for suffering.**

Now perhaps you are reading this and thinking, "Oh, you're so right, Barbara. I know someone who resists the flow of life just like that! But not me. I'm *really* into my growth. Why, I've been working on myself for a long time."

My question for you is: You say you're into *growth*. But are you into *change*? As we've seen, all growth inevitably involves change, and all change challenges our sense of stability. So are you into instability? Does that sound appealing? My honest answer is the same as yours: Definitely not!

At this point, I'm reminded of the anecdote about a middle-aged woman who had always lived a very conservative and careful life. Finding herself depressed, anxious, and in a passionless marriage, she decided, after much resistance, to finally give in and seek psychological counseling. Her first few months of visits with the therapist went very well. The woman asked many questions about the problems in her life, and listened carefully to what the therapist had to say. She diligently did all the homework her therapist asked her to do, reading the suggested books, and even attending some self-help seminars.

One day during their weekly session, the therapist asked the woman to talk about some of the changes she'd made since she began therapy.

"Changes?" the woman replied with a puzzled expression in her voice.

"Yes," the therapist continued, "changes in your behavior, in your attitudes, in the way you communicate with your husband or your children, things like that."

"What changes?" the woman repeated again. "I haven't made any changes."

The therapist took a deep breath before she responded. "Well, Mrs. Adams, if you haven't made any changes, then why do you come here every week?"

"Because I'm into personal growth and working on myself!" Mrs. Adams explained with a straight face. "But I never said anything about actually wanting to change . . ."

How many times have I been working with an individual or a couple who seemed so sincere about their growth, but when I suggested that they actually make a change, I received this same response: "You want me to change? I never said I agreed to change. I said I agreed to work on myself." I am always astonished when I come face to face with this attitude, and yet I understand it completely. We all like the idea of growing. But we don't like the idea of having to go through changes.

This is what I call "conditional growth":

I will grow and work on myself as long as I don't have to change anything major about my life.

I will grow and work on myself as long as I can stay in my comfort zone.

I will grow and work on myself, as long as it doesn't mean I have to reevaluate my marriage/my career/my personal habits/whatever.

**When we go through our lives
with an unconscious agreement to only grow
"conditionally,"
we rob ourselves of so many wonderful
blessings and opportunities
that are waiting for us on the other side of our fear.**

We fear to trust our wings. We plume and feather them, but dare not throw our weight upon them. We cling too often to the perch.
CHARLES B. NEWCOMB

Imagine yourself standing on the edge of a cliff, high above the ground. Across from you, you see another cliff. It is the cliff you want very much to be on. You know you don't want to stay where you are for much longer; you know you've already wasted too much time standing here; you know it's time to jump. Then, just when you think you're ready to leap, you look down at the huge gap of space between the two cliffs, and in that moment, you become overwhelmed with FEAR—fear of falling, fear of not having what it takes to get to the other side, fear of getting there and changing your mind, and not having a way to get back, fear that if you leap, you may have to leave behind something or someone you care deeply about.

Your heart whispers to you of your dreams, reminding you of how badly you want whatever it is that's waiting for you on that other cliff, that you'll never be happy if you stay where you are now, that you've been putting this off for too long already. And you watch other people jumping triumphantly from one side to the other of their own cliffs, calling out to you to do the same. But still, you stand where you are, paralyzed, afraid and unable to leap.

Many times throughout our lives, we find ourselves standing on the edge of a symbolic cliff, knowing that we need to jump over to the cliff on the other side. The first cliff represents who you've been and how you've been living that needs to be changed—the job that you know you need to quit; the relationship that is going nowhere that you know it's time to end; a bad habit or addiction you know you need to overcome. The second cliff represents who you want to be, and what you would like to accomplish—the dream or career you've always wanted to go after; the kind of relationship you've always wished you could have; the risks you've always wanted to take.

Each time you confront these "cliffs" in life, you are offered an opportunity to grow, to become someone better than you were yesterday. But in order to grow, to leap, you have to experience change. And this is where most of us can get stuck.

All growth and accomplishment involves taking a risk,
jumping from one cliff to the next,
leaving your comfort zone
and leaping,
at least temporarily, into the unknown.

Any time we risk changing from who we have been, we enter unfamiliar territory. I'm not just talking about taking enormous risks, like starting your own business or ending a relationship. Your "leap" might be something less overwhelming, but still challenging: the leap from never asking your husband for what you need from him to beginning to express your feelings; the leap from being a behind-the-scenes employee to asking your boss for more responsibility; the leap from being a shy, quiet person to reaching out and making new friends; the leap from wearing the same hairstyle you've had since high school to getting a makeover.

Is it natural for us to feel scared when we contemplate taking these leaps? Sure it is. That first cliff represents your comfort zone. Even though you might be unhappy there, stuck in an unfulfilling career, for instance, or suffering in an unhappy relationship, still, it is *familiar* territory, and your mind interprets what is familiar as *safe*. "Don't jump!" it warns. "You might get hurt! Who knows what could happen? Why take any chances—at least if you stay where you are, you know what to expect."

Resistance to change is one of the most common and deadly ways you may be undermining your growth. Change is necessary for growth; it is unavoidable for growth. In our last chapter, we talked about Secret Number Two: The Purpose of Life Is for You to Grow Into the Best Human Being You Can Be. Secret Number Three logically follows Secret Number Two. It says that the mechanics of growth is the process of change, or, to simplify it even more: If growth is a road that you want to travel, then change is the vehicle you have to use to get from one place to another. And just because it isn't always a comfortable ride doesn't mean you should get out of the car!

Ready or Not, Here Comes Change

To be fully alive, fully human, and completely awake is to be continually thrown out of the nest.
PEMA CHÖDRÖN

Sometimes, even when you know you need to leap, you don't. You stand there on the edge of your cliff, thinking about the changes you should make, talking about the risks you want to take, but doing nothing about it. The longer you wait, the more uncomfortable you feel and the harder it gets to make the decision to go ahead and jump.

And then one day, events that appear to be beyond your control descend upon your life and turn it upside down. Maybe you've been avoiding breaking up with your partner, and suddenly he breaks up with you. Maybe you've been trying to get up the courage to quit your job, and suddenly you are fired. Maybe you've been telling yourself you need to rest more and take better care of yourself, and suddenly you develop an illness. *Whether you like it or not, you are being forced to make the changes you've spent so much energy trying to resist.*

It's as if the evolutionary nature of life, which dictates that all things must continually grow and change in order to exist, saw you standing there on the edge of your cliff, unable to move, and thought, "You know, she is just taking a little too long to get this one on her own. I think that poor girl needs some help!" Suddenly, it's as if a big cosmic boot appears and kicks you off of the cliff! No more waiting. No more procrastinating. All at once, whether you like it or not, you find yourself in midair, flying away from your comfort zone and into the unknown.

I'm sure you're very familiar with "the boot." Speaking for myself, I have many cosmic boot marks on my bottom from times when I've been propelled off my cliffs and forced to go through the very changes I'd been avoiding. What you need to understand about the way the boot works is that it's just doing its job of helping you grow.

There are two ways to grow and change in life:

1. You can choose to grow and change.
2. You can be forced to grow and change.

Secrets Number Two and Three tell us that the purpose of life is to grow, and therefore, change is inevitable. If you don't choose to grow and change on your own, guess what? Cosmic intelligence will "help" you change. It's important to understand, however, that *there is no third option—that you will NOT grow and change. Not growing is not an option.* You will grow, because it is the purpose of your being here. The question is HOW? Will you grow and change willingly, joyfully? Or will you grow and change kicking and screaming the whole way?

Just as I was writing this last section, I received a call from a dear friend. For several years, this woman had been in a very unhealthy, unhappy, on-again, off-again relationship with a man who used and mistreated her in the worst of ways. Those of us who love her have watched her health, happiness, and sense of well-being deteriorate because of the emotionally debilitating effect this guy had on her. Time and time again, hearing her latest complaints about how miserable she was, we would plead with her to break up with him. But in spite of her unusual intelligence, she refused to listen to any of us, or even to her own heart.

When I heard my friend's voice on the phone, I

could have predicted what she was about to say. "He left me, Barbara," she began in a shaky voice, "just like that. He doesn't even want me to contact him. I called to tell you that you were right about him all along."

We spoke for a while and I tried to be as loving and supportive as possible. But do you know what my secret thought was? *"Thank God the universe intervened and gave her the boot."* My friend didn't have the courage or the strength herself to make the leap away from this destructive relationship, so some power greater than her decided to take matters into its own hands, and get this man out of her life. Of course I felt sad that she was in pain, but underneath my concern, I was elated. She wasn't standing on that rotting cliff anymore. She still has a lot of work to do in understanding why she put up with such a poor excuse for a relationship in the first place, but at least she's been forced to finally let go.

I firmly believe that one day this woman will look back and be grateful for the boot she got that lovingly propelled her away from this unhealthy situation. The universe was more committed to her happiness and growth as a soul than she was willing or able to be. It did the work for her that she couldn't do for herself.

The universe is irrevocably committed to your growth.
It will not let you down.
It will remain faithful to your true purpose
in being here
even when you don't.

There is something so very beautiful about this understanding, something profoundly moving and reassuring: even when you resist the life-supportive changes destiny has in store for you and cling to your old cliffs, the benevolent force of growth will remain unwavering in its mission to guide you toward more happiness, more freedom, and will find a way to help you fly.

What to Do When You Want to Leap, But You Don't Feel Ready

As comforting as it is to hear stories of how being booted off of your cliff will be good for you, I think you probably would still find it preferable to jump on your own! So what can you do when you really do want to leap, to surrender to change, but you don't feel *ready*? If there's something you've been wanting to do or a change you've been wanting to make, but you've been stuck up against your own resistance, the following section might be helpful. These are four common reasons your mind will give you for why you're not ready to surrender to change, four mistakes we make in the way we think about change, and four truths or reminders to help you let go and leap.

Reason 1:

I Must Not Be Ready Yet Because I'm Still Afraid

"I want to quit my job, I really do. And I will do it soon, but I'm just not ready. I'm still uncomfortable when I think about doing it. I'll know when the time is right, though, because it won't be such a difficult decision."

"I know I should leave my husband. He'll never stop drinking and I'm totally miserable, but I'm just not ready to do it yet. The thought of being alone just terrifies me, and what if the kids end up hating me for ruining their lives?"

MISTAKE: WE MISINTERPRET OUR FEAR OF LEAPING FOR A LACK OF READINESS. FEAR DOESN'T ALWAYS MEAN YOU AREN'T READY— IT JUST MEANS YOU ARE HUMAN, AND AREN'T COMFORTABLE WITH THE UNKNOWN.

TRUTH: IF YOU WAIT UNTIL YOUR FEAR DIS-APPEARS BEFORE MAKING A CHANGE, YOU WILL PROBABLY WAIT FOREVER!

Reason 2:

I Need More Confidence Before I Can Make a Move

"I really want to start my own business, but I just don't feel confident enough. Maybe if I give it a little more time, I'll feel better and find the courage to do it."

"I know I should stop dating my boyfriend, because the relationship has been awful for months, but I don't feel confident enough to believe that I will ever be able to find anyone else. Maybe if I give myself some more time to get used to the idea, I will feel better about it."

MISTAKE: WE MISINTERPRET OUR LACK OF CONFIDENCE ABOUT MAKING A CHANGE AS A SIGN THAT WE AREN'T READY TO DO IT. YOUR LACK OF CONFIDENCE COMES FROM THE FACT THAT YOU'RE VENTURING INTO NEW TERRITORY.

TRUTH: YOU NEVER GAIN TRUE CONFIDENCE IN YOUR ABILITY TO DO SOMETHING UNTIL YOU ACTUALLY DO IT!

Reason 3:

This Isn't the Right Time to Do It

"I know I need to talk to my husband about the problems we are having, but this really isn't a very good time. The kids just got over the flu and my mother-in-law is coming to visit next week. I'll do it soon, really I will, just not now."

"I want to write that novel I've always dreamed of, but this is a bad time to be an author. The market is full of novels about that topic, and I think I should wait a few years until there is more of a demand."

MISTAKE: WE HIDE FROM OUR FEAR OF MAKING A CHANGE BY TELLING OURSELVES THAT IT ISN'T THE "RIGHT TIME" TO LEAP. MAKING CHANGES ALWAYS FORCES YOU TO LEAVE YOUR COMFORT ZONE, AND SO OF COURSE IT WILL NEVER FEEL LIKE THE RIGHT TIME TO TAKE A RISK.

TRUTH: ONLY AFTER YOU FIND THE COURAGE TO MAKE A CHANGE AND EXPERIENCE ITS BENEFITS WILL IT *FEEL* "RIGHT," BECAUSE YOUR FEAR WILL FINALLY BE GONE.

Reason 4:

I'm Not Sure If I Really Want to Do It Anyway

"I know I've always wanted to open my own clothing store. But lately I've been thinking that perhaps I am not as committed to the idea as I should be. I must have just gotten excited about it because of my friend's success, but I'm not sure it's really the right thing for me. Perhaps I should just keep my present job."

"I know I've been saying I need to get a divorce, that my husband and I have nothing in common, and haven't had a sex life in years. But maybe I'm just being unrealistic, and this is the way marriage is supposed to be. Things aren't that bad, between us. I mean, how important is sex anyway? Perhaps I could be happy living this way."

MISTAKE: WHEN WE FEEL AFRAID OF MAKING A CHANGE, WE FOOL OURSELVES INTO BELIEVING THAT WE REALLY DON'T WANT TO DO IT ANYWAY.

TRUTH: YOU WILL ALWAYS DOUBT THE VALIDITY OF YOUR NEW PATH UNTIL YOU SEE WHERE IT TAKES YOU!

I'm sure some of these sound familiar to you—they do to me! How do you think I came up with them? For years, I've watched my own mind resist the changes I wanted to make in my life by using these and many other supposedly logical "reasons" whose purpose was to convince me to stay right where I was in my comfort zone. I'm not saying you should go ahead and unconditionally make every change in your life you've been wanting to make by tomorrow. But if you've been going back and forth about taking a leap, and one of these reasons sounds awfully familiar, you might want to use the truths I've listed as a way to navigate yourself out of the labyrinth of your own fear.

The Power of Surrendering and Letting Go

Instead of seeing the rug being pulled from under us,
we can learn to dance on a shifting carpet.
THOMAS CRUM

So how do we stop resisting? How do we let go of our tight hold on the way we think things are supposed to be and begin to surrender to life's flow?

We need to learn how to make
friends with the unknown.

Isn't that what's so scary about change? *We are afraid of the unknown.* I'm afraid to leap because I don't know what is waiting for me on that new cliff. At least I know where I'm standing now. At least I'm familiar with my pain, my unhappiness, my lack of contentment. But if I leave this behind, who knows what could happen?

This is the same dilemma we all go through every time we are confronted with change: **We come face to face with the gap, the void, the unknown.**

- I want to start a new business, but first I have to quit my job.
- I want to find a new, healthy relationship, but first I have to end the relationship I'm in.
- I want to buy a new house, but first I have to sell the house I own.

Now if God could just promise you: "You'll be out of work for six weeks, but at that point you'll get all the financing to start your own business," then you could quit. Or, "You'll be single for four months, two weeks, and five days, but then you'll meet the most amazing man, and in fact, here's a picture of him," well, you'd break up with your boyfriend in a heartbeat. If someone could just show you what's coming, why, you could take the most outrageous leaps in your life, right?

I call this **the desire for a cosmic bridge.** How wonderful it would be if each time we needed to make a change, we were easily and calmly ushered over a bridge of circumstances or opportunities that instantly connected us to our new and happy future! What a relief it would be if we were given a map, an itinerary, and a timetable detailing exactly what would happen between letting go of one thing and receiving another!

But that's not the way it works. You're often asked to go through changes without knowing the outcome, to let go of one thing before you have been given another, to cross over without a bridge. And that's where it gets scary—in the gap, in the space between.

> The gap between two things is a place of great potential,
> a place of great power.
> But it's also a place that can bring you face to face with your greatest fears.

What if I end this relationship, but I never meet anyone else for the rest of my life?

What if I quit this job, but no one ever offers me a job again?

What if I move out of this house, but I never find another nice place to live?

What if I distance myself from these old friends who I don't really enjoy anymore, but I never make any new friends?

What if I let go of what I'm holding onto, but nothing else good ever comes to me?

> *What if I move into the gap, and I get stuck there*
> *forever?*

It's this fear of getting stuck in the gap between what we are holding onto and what we hope will come that prevents many of us from ever letting go.

The Power of Letting Go

Imagine that you had a special gift to give someone, but when you approached her, you saw that her arms were full of packages. What would you do? You wouldn't say, "Here," and leave the gift on the ground. You wouldn't put it on her head. You would wait until she let go of her packages, and then present the gift to her.

The universe operates in this same way. The universe is intelligent, and it's not wasteful. The universe doesn't try to give you something when your hands are full. It doesn't pile something on top of you when you're already holding too much. It waits until you've made room, until you're ready to receive—then it can put something in your hands. But that means in order for you to receive something new, you may have to let go of what you're holding on to.

Have you ever watched a trapeze artist at the circus flying high above the ground? She holds tightly to the bar of the trapeze, swinging her body in graceful and powerful motions, and then, just as she approaches the second trapeze, she lets go. For a second, she is suspended in the air with nothing to hold on to, and the crowd gasps. Then, she reaches for the bar swinging toward her and grabs it just in time. We are mesmerized when we witness this feat of courage and daring. It is such an extreme physical example of the need to let go of one thing before we can really receive another.

When you let go of something, you create a vacuum. One of the most basic principles of Nature is that the universe abhors a vacuum. If water is in a pond and you dig a new trough at the edge of the pond leading five feet away, will the water remain where it is? No, it will flow into the new space and fill up the vacuum. If a fire is raging in one area, and the firefighters remove the barrier that is keeping it contained, will the fire politely stay where it is? No, it's going to move into whatever vacuum it can find.

In terms of our emotional and spiritual growth, this principle says that when you create some emptiness, some space, it will be filled up with something new. But first you have to clean out the old. You have to let go.

> Letting go of what no longer serves you
> opens you up to receive all the new gifts
> life has waiting for you.

When you feel you have hit a block of resistance in your life, that things are stagnant and nothing new is coming in, it's time for you to get rid of something. *You need to symbolically move the energy to make space for the new.* How can you do this? Clean out your closet, give away clothing you're not wearing, throw away old papers that are cluttering your drawers and closets, donate some money to a worthy cause, do some inner work to eliminate old mental and emotional concepts that are no longer serving your growth. Create some space. Of course, our tendency when we feel not much is coming into our lives is to do the opposite, to hold on more tightly to what we already have, but this only will slow your process down. *Remember: The universe abhors a vacuum.*

How I Let Go of the Old and Attracted the New

For the past few years, I had been thinking about selling my home in Southern California. I loved my house very much and had lived in it for quite a while, but something powerful inside of me felt it was time to move on, and that I should rent a home until I figured out what new direction my life was about to take. This made sense to my mind, but not to my heart. I was so attached to this house—it was my comfort zone, my safe haven away from the world. How could I let go of it, especially if I didn't know where I would be going?

Fortunately, I had a very compassionate real estate agent, who listened patiently as I explained my dilemma: I did want to sell my house, but I was afraid I wouldn't find anything to rent that would make me happy. What if my house sold, and I had to move out and still had no place to go? What if the kind of place I wanted to rent didn't really exist, and I should rethink the whole idea of selling in the first place? Obviously, I was terrified of making the leap.

"Barbara," the agent said, "I understand your concerns. But you can't rent a new place before you sell your house. First you sell, then you look."

"I know," I replied, "but before I can officially put my house on the market, I have to get more information. So I thought I'd spend a few weeks checking out houses that are available to be leased, not to actually rent them yet, but just to prove to myself that they exist. Then, I'll calm down, and be able to tell you to go ahead and sell this one."

Even as I heard myself trying to explain this tactic to my realtor, I knew what I was doing—I was trying to find a bridge between those two cliffs. It would be as if you were in an unhappy relationship and you wanted to leave your husband, but you were afraid there were no eligible men out there for you to meet. So you decide, "I'm going to put an ad in the paper pretending I'm single, and I'll get phone calls and the pictures so I can see who's available. I won't actually date anyone. I just want to know that they're out there, and once I'm reassured, then I'll leave my husband." That's what I was thinking—I wanted to see some houses and then I'd know they were there and I'd calm down. I should have suspected that the universe wasn't going to let me get away with this blatant attempt to control the flow of events and avoid my lessons.

My realtor did agree to my unusual plan, and for one month she took me to see every house for rent that she could find. And it was awful! Nothing was even close to what I needed or what I liked. One house would be too dark, one would have no privacy, one wouldn't take dogs, and each one seemed worse than the last. As the days passed, I grew more and more anxious. And so did my realtor. "Barbara," she reminded me, "if you don't put your house on the market now, you will have to wait until after the holidays, and that's months away."

"But I'm too scared to sell my house without knowing I've found something," I'd reply. And even as I said it, I could hear a voice in my head responding, *"But you won't find something until you let go of what you're holding on to."*

Surrender and let go. I'd been writing this for weeks. Did I really believe that I was going to be let off the hook on this one? God was basically saying to me, "Look, Barbara, you're not in spiritual elementary school, you're not in spiritual junior high school, you're in spiritual graduate school, and there is no way are you going to be pampered through this. You need to trust me."

Finally, I surrendered. I knew I needed to let go of control, to just say, "God, I trust you to provide the perfect situation and make the perfect set of events happen." It was time to let go of the house. So I got up all my strength, called my realtor, and said, "O.K., today is the day—I'm signing the papers. I'm taking the leap."

My relieved realtor rushed over and we sat outside in my backyard as I signed the papers giving her permission to list my house for sale. She thanked me and left, and I was alone gazing out at the mountains across the canyon. "What have I done?" I thought morosely. "I'm letting go of something so beautiful, and I'll probably never find a place to rent where I'll be happy." But I had taken the leap, and I knew that at this point I just had to trust.

I opened the local newspaper and began browsing through the real estate section to see how much other houses were selling for. Suddenly, an ad caught my eye: "Gorgeous house with view for rent." The cynical part of me thought, "Yeah, right, it's probably a dump like all the other places I've seen." The ad gave a private phone number, not a realty firm, which made me even more suspicious. Most likely, the owner was too embarrassed to even show the house to a realtor. But something told me to call and inquire about the house anyway. "What do I have to lose?" I thought. I dialed the number.

A French woman answered the phone, and when I asked about the house, she told me she'd just finished remodeling it, and that, in fact, it was right down the street from me. She described it in glowing terms, and I was sure she had to be exaggerating, but agreed to meet her there the next day.

As I parked my car in front of the house the next morning, I braced myself for yet another disappointment. The house didn't look like much from the outside. I saw a car pull up and a woman got out who looked like she could be my sister. It was the owner. She greeted me with a smile, and we walked up to the front door and entered.

My mouth hung open in amazement. It was as if this woman had taken my home and built a scaled-down version of it. It was gorgeous, and as she took me from room to room, I shook my head in disbelief. Everything was exactly as I would have wanted it—the colors, the view, the kind of doors and windows I liked. She had even constructed a new master bathroom that used the exact fixtures that I had in my bathroom. And she'd created a closet that could actually hold all of my clothes!

"This is too good to be true," I thought. "Maybe there is something wrong with it." But the more we talked, the more I liked her and the more my heart whispered, "This is your new house!"

I told her I would think about it and drove home, just two minutes up the hill! I could hardly believe it. It seemed too perfect, too easy. But I thought about it all the next day, and knew that I wanted this house. I left a message on the owner's machine and told her to call me.

My experience is that when we start to question grace, when we doubt the gifts the universe is trying to give us, it's as if the universe says, *"Okay, this is too comfortable for you? Well, then we'll stir things up if that will make you happier. You weren't due for a challenge for two more weeks, but I'll create one if you insist. You're the one writing the script."*

The next morning, the woman called me at home and explained that she would love to rent her house to me, but that I would have to take it by a certain date which was fast approaching. "But I haven't sold my house yet," I explained worriedly. "Is there any way that you can wait a little longer?"

"I don't think so," she replied. "The house is almost ready, and I need to rent it. So you think about it."

"Here it comes," I thought. "The house was just perfect, and now it's being snatched away from me." I watched my fear and resistance begin to emerge, and suddenly caught myself. "No, I *have* to surrender and trust. I can't stop now."

And so I prayed that night, and thanked God for finding me the perfect house so quickly after I had released my old one, but mentioned I needed a little more help. "If this is supposed to be my house," I asked, "please create a delay so she can't rent it yet. Please make something go wrong that will need to be fixed."

I was sitting at my computer working on this book when the phone rang in the morning. It was the owner of the house. "Barbara," she began, "you won't believe what has happened. I just had the house inspected, and there's a problem with some of the construction that needs to be redone. It means I won't be able to rent it for a few more months. When the inspector told me this, my first thought was, 'It must be because Barbara is meant to have this house.' "

When I hung up the phone, I had tears of gratitude in my eyes. I could almost see God smiling with satisfaction as if to say, "My dear, what is your problem? How much do I have to prove to you that when you let go, you will always receive, that when you surrender, grace will always take over and give you what you really need?"

Within a short time my old house sold, and now I am living in that new house, the house to which I was led only moments after letting go of what I'd been holding on to so tightly.

Making Room for Grace

Learning to let go begins to make room for grace. What is grace? It's that life-bestowing, love-bestowing power of the universe, the mysterious way cosmic intelligence has of moving you toward more goodness, more truth, more freedom. When we resist change, hold on too tightly, and refuse to let go, grace cannot easily enter our lives.

I believe that God, spirit, the universal power, or whatever you call it for yourself has so much to give you, but only if you cooperate. Are you doing your part? Maybe the universe is just working overtime for you, but you are not letting in the blessings. Maybe there's a big pile of blessings waiting for you in some cosmic storehouse, but they can't come into your life until you make the space. You may be praying, you may be doing affirmations, you may be going to therapy, attending twelve-step program meetings, reading uplifting books—but are you really cooperating by letting go of what's not serving you anymore?

Make room for grace—on the physical level as well as the emotional level. Find the courage to let go of whatever doesn't serve you anymore, whether it's a relationship, your job, old possessions, or beliefs and emotions you've been clinging to.

A wonderful contemplation to help you with this is to ask yourself:

> **What is it that I've been holding on to that I need to let go of?**
> **What is no longer serving me in my life that I need to release?**

I know that it's scary to let go. But your fear that by letting go, you will end up with nothing, is groundless. Deep inside, you know this. You have no evidence in your life that this is the way things turn out. So many times when you thought you were losing something valuable, something much greater has come along. So many times when you were forced to let go of something you thought you couldn't live without, you've ended up with something far better than you had ever imagined was possible.

> *Every exit is an entry into somewhere else.*
> TOM STOPPARD

There's a wonderful exercise you can use to help remind yourself that change has been a benevolent force in your life. On the left side of a piece of paper, make a list of every time you've let go of something, or someone, willingly or unwillingly. Start from the time you were a teenager, and continue into your adult years. For instance:

1. Broke up with boyfriend when I was sixteen.
2. Didn't get into the college my best friend was going to.
3. Got fired from my job as an assistant to a photographer in my junior year.
4. Had to move out of my apartment when they sold the building.

Then, next to each item, see if you can write down something that came along and replaced what you had lost. It may not have come right away, or in a way that you expected it to, but you will find that something *did* come, and in most cases, it was something better than what you'd had before.

This exercise can give you an astonishing perspective that your life truly is always growing and moving toward more. And when you're done, you will have an amazing list of blessings, surprises, and even miracles on the right side of the page!

Show Me

There is a design for you and your life that is bigger than anything you could imagine. If you can just let go a little and allow the flow to move you along, you will be delivered into more joy and contentment than you could ever imagine was possible. Learning to surrender to life's flow is almost like unlearning so many of the ways you normally deal with reality. Stop resisting, stop controlling, stop manipulating, and pay attention to the changes that are being presented to you. Find the current of the river and let it take you where you need to go.

When we understand that the nature of life is change,
we can stop resisting the inevitable changes,
big and small,
and learn to surrender
to the natural movement in our inner and
outer world.

Recently I had lunch with a wonderful friend and an inspiring writer, Clarissa Pinkola Estes, who wrote the impactful book *Women Who Run with the Wolves*. We were having one of those magical conversations women have, where wisdom seems to pour out of us and we are each adding our own delicious ingredients to a delightful emotional and spiritual "stew" of ideas. I shared with her that I was in the middle of writing this book for women, and we began discussing the topic of surrender.

"I've really been working on controlling less and surrendering more," I confessed to Clarissa. "I think I used to get up each morning with an inner attitude that said to the universe: 'O.K., I don't want any funny business today. I don't want any surprises. You know the agenda, so let's just stick to it and everything will be fine.' It was almost as if I was giving the day a warning: **Don't mess with me!**

"In the past few years," I continued, "I began to realize that by doing that, I was cutting myself off from grace. I know that there is a powerful force of divine energy flowing through our lives everyday, like a river of grace. Having that 'Don't mess with me' attitude is like saying, 'I'm not getting in the river. I'm not getting wet. You can try to get me wet all you want, but I'm going to sit here on the riverbank.' By trying so hard to control what happened during my day, I was actually robbing myself of the magic each day had to offer me."

Clarissa smiled in agreement and shared a story with me: "At one point in my life," she began, "I was going through one of those really difficult times. I felt lost. I had no idea what I was supposed to do. So I prayed to the Blessed Mother. 'Help me!' I pleaded with her. 'Give me the answers I'm looking for. Tell me what to do!'

"Then," Clarissa continued, "I sat down to meditate. And suddenly, the Blessed Mother appeared before me and said just one word: *Enseñame*. It's a Spanish phrase which means 'show me.' She was telling me that this was to be my prayer, this was the answer—to ask the universe to show me. I had prayed for a solution to my problem and had wanted some long manifesto as my response, and, preferably, also someone to come and take my hand and dance me all the way through the whole dance. Instead, I got one word!"

Enseñame. Show me. A prayer to the Goddess, to the

Universal Mother, to the Great Intelligence. *"Show me what I need to learn. Show me what I need to let go of. Show me the path to take. Show me whatever you want to show me. Show me how I can serve. Show me new ways to love."*

Clarissa told me that she starts the day with this word. What a beautiful way to begin each day, with a conscious act of surrender! I confessed to her that I, too, begin my day in a similar manner, with a prayer from an ancient Sanskrit text that offers all of my thoughts and actions to God, and to the service of love. And as we sat there eating our lunch, I couldn't help but smile to think about all of the women who have read Clarissa's books, and my books, and how surprised some of them might be to discover that we both start our day by calling out to the universal power and say: "I know I am not doing any of this on my own. Show me what I am meant to do."

Taking a moment each morning before you jump into your daily activity to open yourself up to a higher power than your own thoughts, your own fears, and your own limited vision will allow you to resist life less and flow more. Whether your prayer is in Sanskrit or Spanish or English or simply the wordless language of the heart, it will act as an invitation for grace to enter in. Ask for guidance, ask for signs, ask for direction, and it *will* come.

I try to remember to practice consciously surrendering, not just in the morning, but throughout my day, especially when I notice that I am experiencing some inner or outer resistance. Just a few days ago, I found myself up against an obstacle I couldn't see my way around. I was having a problem figuring out how to communicate some important feelings to a person for whom I care deeply. Nothing I tried worked—in fact, the harder I tried, the worse things got between us. At one point I found myself sitting on the floor of my office with my head in my hands thinking, "I give up! I just can't figure it out. I don't know what to do."

Suddenly, I heard myself, and knew that I was actually doing the exact thing I needed to do: I was surrendering, releasing my attempt to control or fix the situation by myself. A prayer formed in my heart:

"Show me what to do. Show me how I am supposed to move through this."

Instantly, I felt better. Nothing on the outside had changed, but I had stopped resisting. And within a few hours, an amazing thing happened: the answers I hadn't been able to find for days began appearing in the form of friends who called and gave me helpful advice, as well as inner guidance that gently steered me toward a new way of thinking about my problem. Later that night when I spoke again to the person with whom I'd been having the problem, it seemed that I had somehow found a way to express my feelings so that he could understand them, and also to successfully convey to him my compassion for his point of view. Just like that, the obstacle between us had vanished.

Learn to call upon the magic of grace to show you the way. Even if you don't believe in it, try it. You'll be amazed at what happens. Whenever you feel like you've temporarily lost your sense of direction or have cut yourself off from the current of goodness, don't panic. Just resist a little bit less, flow a little bit more, ask for help, and you'll be amazed at where you'll be taken.

Now Is the Moment You've Been Waiting for

Hell begins on the day when God grants us a clear vision of all that we might have achieved, of all the gifts which we have wasted, of all that we might have done which we did not do. For me the conception of hell lies in two words: TOO LATE.
GIAN-CARLO MENOTTI, COMPOSER

When is the right moment for you to begin surrendering to the changes that are already beginning to unfold in your life, the changes you know you need to make? *Now.* Now is the moment you've been waiting for. It is the perfect moment. There is no better moment.

You can take a really bold approach and actually invite change into your life. Just put out an invitation to the universe:

I am opening myself to receiving whatever growth and changes you have in store for me.

You can also go inside and tap into your own inner wisdom that is waiting to point you in the right direction. To do this, take a few deep breaths until you feel your body begin to relax. Let all the tension go. Now, ask yourself these questions:

> "In what area of my life right now do I feel the need for some change?"
> "What area has been trying to change, but I've been resisting?"

Did you hear some answers? Of course you did. You see, you already know these things. You know the areas where change is trying to invite you to dance with it. So accept the invitation. When you release your tight hold on life, it will move and flow in new directions and take you to increasingly deeper levels of joy and fulfillment. It's only going to lead you to something greater. It's only going to lead you to something more.

Find the courage you need to leap. You may not be ready to take your biggest leap. That's okay. Start out with small ones. But leap now!

> *A ship in harbor is safe—*
> *but that's not what ships are for.*
> JOHN A. SHEDD

A few nights ago, I discovered a spider trapped behind some wooden molding in the corner of my bedroom. The spider was moving very slowly, as if it had been stuck there for a long time, unable to nourish itself. "Don't worry, little one," I said in a soft voice, "I'll get you out of here."

I took a tissue in my hand, and attempted to gently scoop up the spider so I could put it outside in the garden. But the spider obviously thought I was trying to attack it and ran back into the molding. "I won't hurt you," I promised, trying again to lift the spider up. And again the spider fought me, wildly waving its legs, rolling into a ball, and trying to smash itself into the molding.

Suddenly, I noticed that the spider wasn't moving. I peered at it closely and saw that it had resisted so strongly that it had killed itself. Sadly, I took the spider outside and placed it on the dirt near a rose bush. "I wasn't trying to hurt you," I whispered softly. "I was just trying to save you. I'm sorry you didn't know that."

In that moment, I had an amazing thought: "Is this how God feels about me, about all of us?" Perhaps that loving force of cosmic intelligence sees us struggling, suffering, in trouble, and intervenes in an attempt to move us out of danger to safety, but we resist, kicking and screaming and complaining, and wondering why we are being forced to change. Perhaps we are just like that spider, who mistook a rescue mission for an attack, not realizing that if he had simply surrendered to the ride, he would have found himself in a beautiful garden.

·   ·   ·

Changes are calling to you.
   Can you hear them?
Doors that have been closed are opening wide.
   Can you see them?
New pathways are appearing right before your eyes
   Will you follow them?

As it says in the Talmud:
   "And if not now, when?"

All Obstacles Are Lessons in Disguise— Honor Them and Learn from Them

*The perfect problems
lead to the perfect freedom.*

GURUMAYI CHIDVILASANANDA

What if you knew for sure that every single event that happened to you while you were alive was part of a great plan to make you into the most loving, strong, wise human being possible?

What if you knew for sure that each apparent problem or difficulty was actually a blessing in disguise, an opportunity for tremendous growth that could not happen otherwise?

What if you understood that your obstacles, rather than being your worst enemies, were actually your dearest friends? Then how would you treat your obstacles? What attitude would you have toward them?

Right now, you probably are facing some obstacles. Maybe they're obstacles in your intimate relationship; maybe they're obstacles at work; maybe they're obstacles with a family member; maybe they are obstacles with money or your health. You probably believe if you could just snap your fingers and make your obstacles vanish once and for all, you would be so much happier. *You may even think that the presence of those obstacles indicates that you are doing something wrong, or that something is wrong with you.*

This is one of the mistakes we make in the way we approach our life: We think that our obstacles and challenges are "bad" things that we should get rid of as quickly as possible, just as you'd want to take out a bag of smelly trash. When we have this attitude about our obstacles, each challenge and problem becomes the enemy that we fight against. *We live in a constant battle with our own destiny.* No wonder we often feel stressed out, exhausted, and unhappy. We have placed ourselves in an unnecessary war with life itself.

It is tempting to react this way to our challenges. After all, who would actually *choose* to go through a difficult time in a relationship, or to experience financial hardship, or to be faced with a serious crisis of any kind? However, when you treat your obstacles as adversaries, you never get close enough to them to discover the gifts they are actually bearing. You never look deeply enough into them to see the opportunity they offer you to learn important lessons.

When you only view your obstacles as undesirable, you rob yourself of the hidden lessons they contain.

Remember: The earth is a big classroom. What we've been addressing in these chapters is that the purpose of life is for you to grow, that change is inevitable, that things aren't always supposed to be easy. Obstacles will always be a part of this life. I believe that one of the qualities that most defines us as human beings is *how* we handle these obstacles and challenges.

Creating a successful life doesn't mean waking up one morning and being able to say: "Finally, no more challenges, no more obstacles, no more adversity." The existence of obstacles in your life isn't the issue—how you deal with your obstacles when they arise *is* the issue.

The Hidden Gift in Your Problems

A few months ago, I was attending a meditation intensive with my spiritual teacher and she brought up the topic of how each of us faces challenges in life. She recounted a story which I want to share with you.

"Once some people brought a man to meet me for the first time," she began. "This man was introduced and proudly announced that he had just returned from visiting a special magic yogi in India. 'This yogi told me that he could perform a certain spell,' the man explained, 'and in doing so, he was going to take away all my karma, all my obstacles, and all my problems. And so he performed the spell, and now I am sure I will never have any problems ever again!'

Then my teacher said to us, "When I heard this story, I sent a special prayer to my guru saying, 'Thank God you never did that to me! How would I have ever learned compassion and trust and patience and faith if I hadn't had obstacles?'"

Isn't this a beautiful and wise attitude—to actually be thankful for our obstacles and all of the opportunities they offer us to grow? Obstacles are an inevitable part of the way life molds us. Indeed, they are put in our path to be our greatest teachers.

If we did not have problems, we would never learn
strength.
If we did not have struggles, we would never learn
resilience.
If we did not have delays, we would never learn
patience.
If we did not have resistance, we would never learn
perseverance.
If we did not have hopelessness, we would never learn
faith.
If we did not have suffering, we would never learn
compassion.

Think about your own life for a moment. How did you
learn your most important lessons? How did you develop
your greatest strengths, the most essential parts of your
character? It was probably from having to undergo hardship, having to face problems. I'm not crazy about this
fact of life, either, but it's undeniable:

We grow most from difficulties,
and not as much from good times.

I know a man who grew up in a very privileged, protected
environment and until his early twenties had a very easy
life. He was given all the money he wanted, he was never
chastised for any kind of misbehavior, he was never expected to work, and was basically spoiled in every way
possible. "I don't understand why so many people whine

about their lives, why they need all this counseling and self-help stuff," he would exclaim. "Life is great." Easy for him to say!

This man graduated from college and went out into the world to get a job. He found a position with a prestigious company and within just a few days, the "you know what" hit the fan. All of a sudden, he wasn't protected anymore. He couldn't handle criticism or take feedback. He couldn't handle any of his ideas being rejected. The simplest opposition or problem would knock him over because he did not have the inner strength and resources to deal with any challenges whatsoever. He had never been confronted with obstacles and so he had never learned any skills for staying afloat when the water gets rough. He quit his job after only one week.

That was five years ago. I recently heard that this guy is still going from job to job, from career to career, and whenever things get difficult, he bails out, blaming his business partners or the economy or a variety of other factors for his problems. His parents are good people who were only trying to provide their son with the best, but in removing all possible obstacles in his path, they unintentionally crippled him so that he is incapable of facing any kind of difficulty.

Whenever I think of this story, I feel a sudden rush of gratitude for all of the obstacles I've faced in my life, and there have been plenty! As much as I have bemoaned them at the time, each one has made me stronger and more courageous and has deepened my faith in the perfection of the mysterious way in which the universe works. *If this is the case, shouldn't we all be honoring our obstacles instead of cursing them?*

This is the fourth principle:

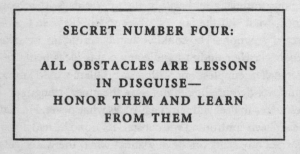

SECRET NUMBER FOUR:

ALL OBSTACLES ARE LESSONS
IN DISGUISE—
HONOR THEM AND LEARN
FROM THEM

All problems, all obstacles are gifts in disguise. Hidden within them are the exact lessons your soul needs to learn. Seeing obstacles as lessons invites you to shift your way of thinking about problems and adversity, to assume a cosmic point of view rather than a limited one, to see your life through God's eyes rather than just your own eyes. Then, you can honor the challenges and even welcome them as the very events and circumstances which will help you grow the most.

How Obstacles Teach You About Yourself

There was a great Sufi saint, a woman named Rabi'a al Adawiyya, who said:

> "May God steal from you all that steals you
> from Him."

What steals us from God, from connection with our own spirit? It is our fear, our mistrust, our pride, our cynicism, our lack of faith, the very emotions and attitudes we often experience when we are in crisis. So how does God steal these back? *Perhaps by putting obstacles in our path that will force us to confront these qualities within ourselves, and to begin healing them.*

> There is nothing more effective in showing us
> where we are stuck, where we need to grow,
> and what lessons we need to learn
> than the obstacles that cross our path.

A few years ago, I was in the middle of what seemed to be a massive attack on my life by one obstacle after another. I felt totally overwhelmed by an unending army of insoluble problems, and each day I watched myself slipping deeper and deeper into a state of panic and despair. One afternoon, I drove down to the beach near my house, hoping to find some peace and inspiration from the ocean, which has always had a healing influence on my heart.

There was no one else on the stretch of beach when I arrived. I sat down in the sand near the water and began to watch the waves breaking upon the shore. Suddenly, I felt a surge of anger rising up from deep inside of me. Perhaps it was the sound of the crashing waves that reminded me of how I, too, felt pounded by life, or perhaps

I'd finally reached my emotional limit, for tears began to pour from my eyes and I began to shout: "I HATE THIS! I HATE THIS!" For several minutes, I roared, and the sea roared back.

Finally, I stopped yelling and crying and rested my head on my knees, closing my swollen eyes. And then, as clear as can be, I heard a strong, calm voice from within me say:

**When you HATE what is happening,
know something marvelous is happening,
something important, something life-changing.**

I repeated this phrase to myself in amazement: When you hate what is happening, know something marvelous is happening, something important, something life-changing. It was as if God had heard me shouting: "I HATE THIS!" as I thought about all of my obstacles, and answered: "You hate what is happening? Why, I'm delighted to hear it! It's an excellent sign that important work is taking place and essential lessons are being learned. If you didn't hate it this much, then I'd be worried."

I sat up straight once more and began to contemplate what it actually was about the difficult events in my life that I hated so much. "Why do I hate what is happening?" I asked myself. The answer came in a second:

"Because it makes me feel scared, betrayed, out of control, confused, mistrustful, insecure, helpless, inadequate, and stuck."

Yuck! No wonder I hated the obstacles that were confronting me—they were very effectively luring every undesirable emotion out of my psyche. So was it the actual obstacles I hated? *No, it was what they were uncovering that had been lurking inside of me long before the specific incidents ever occurred.*

From this point of view, I had to admit how efficiently these particular problems were processing me, revealing emotional wounds and attitudes that I needed to address and heal. These obstacles were like a surgeon's knife, slicing me open and exposing the diseased tissue so it could be cut out. Surgery is painful and it is bloody, but it removes that which is unhealthy and life-threatening. Yes, I hated what was happening, but now I could see that it was teaching me some essential lessons about myself and how I needed to grow.

> Obstacles show you where you are stuck.
> They show you where you haven't mastered stuff.
> They push every button you have.
> They don't play fair.
> They hit below the belt.
> They use scary tactics to get your attention.
> They force you to wake up when you have been
>   asleep, to confront what you have been
>   avoiding, to face what you don't want to face.

There's a reason when you are faced with an obstacle, you often say:

"I can't believe this is happening to me!"

No kidding! If you could believe it, it wouldn't be such a big deal and therefore, it wouldn't be an effective obstacle delivering a powerful lesson!

When you look back on your life,
the most profound days
will *not* be the days when nothing happened.
They will be the days when you said,
"I can't believe this is happening!"

How Pain Wakes Us Up

Everything in our life can wake us up or put us to sleep,
and basically it's up to us to let it wake us up.
PEMA CHÖDRÖN

One of the ways our obstacles teach us is through pain. It could be the pain of loss, the pain of jealousy, the pain of rejection, the pain of disappointment, the pain of disillusionment. There are so many kinds of pain and each contains its own particular lessons.

No matter what kind of pain you experience, the impact that pain has on you will be the same:

Pain wakes you up when you have been asleep.
It forces you to pay immediate attention.
It drives you to look deeper into the truth.

Can you recall a time in your life when something happened that caused you tremendous pain? There was no escape—the pain was all around you, forcing you to stay focused on whatever your obstacle or difficulty was. But when you stayed with the pain, because you had to, you began to delve more deeply into the problem and suddenly, you experienced insights and revelations you hadn't expected. It's as if the pain held you down in one spot long enough for you to see the truth that was right in front of your eyes.

I just had an experience of this while I was writing this chapter. Several days ago, I had a very difficult and painful conversation with someone I love very much. This person gave me all kinds of feedback about how I'd been communicating with him in ways that didn't make him feel loved. I was astonished to hear this and was certain that he had somehow misunderstood me. We agreed to talk more later that day.

Well, that day passed and so did the next, with one obstacle after another preventing this conversation from happening. By the third day, I was experiencing a lot of emotional pain. I hadn't had a chance to "fix" things with this person, to explain myself. What if he pulled away permanently? What if we lost the closeness we had always experienced? My mind began to imagine one horrible scenario after another and I became more and more miserable. No matter what I did, I couldn't get the pain to stop. And still, no phone call.

Obstacles are lessons in disguise. Honor them and learn from them. There were the words on the top of the very page I was editing. I knew too much to kid myself into believing that this incident just "happened" to be taking place while I was writing this particular chapter. I knew I was being given an opportunity, or more accurately, being forced to take the opportunity to put what I was teaching into practice. And so I began to shift my attitude about what was going on. "There is a wonderful lesson in this," I reassured myself. Of course, I couldn't see the lesson yet and I still felt awful, but I figured I better start looking for the lesson or I'd never finish this chapter!

The first thing I did was to move completely into my pain. What does that mean? Well, usually when you're in emotional pain, what do you do? Anything you can to avoid it, to numb it, to make it go away. *You make the pain the enemy and either run from it, or attack it with whatever weapons you're used to employing in your psychic battles—alcohol, food, drugs, watching television, shopping, keeping yourself busy, and many others.* Moving into your pain means to go toward it, rather than away from it, to actually embrace it.

Pema Chödrön, a Buddhist nun and the author of one of my favorite books, *When Things Fall Apart*, says this about facing our pain, our difficulty: *"If we run away from challenges, we only prevent ourselves from growing. We may think we have escaped pain, but we have only resisted awakening. Pain does not come from a person or place or event; it is created in the mind. As long as we run from the thing that we resist, the pain stays in the mind. When we face the object of our difficulty, only then do we have an opportunity to free ourselves."*

It was time to face my pain. I sat down, closed my eyes, and felt the sensation of pain in my body, especially in my heart. I let the pain wash over me, like tidal waves of powerful energy. I let the tears come, without worrying about what they meant. I let myself feel all of the emotions that arose—anger, fear, grief, love, longing. Some of these emotions were from current relationships. Some I recognized from past relationships and as far back as my childhood. I allowed myself to experience whatever came up without judging it or resisting it.

After some time, I became aware that the pain had subsided and I felt more stillness, as if a storm had passed. I got up, blew my nose, and went back to work. But over the next few hours, I noticed something amazing. I began to have a series of astonishing revelations about my conversation with this friend and to hear what he'd been saying from a totally different point of view. It was as if someone had just handed me a book with pages full of information about myself, my patterns, and my unconscious thoughts, and I suddenly understood what had been happening and what I needed to learn from the situation. Whereas before my mind had been clouded with fears and anxieties, now it seemed a wind had blown all of these away, and my awareness was crystal clear. The more lessons I uncovered for myself, the lighter I felt.

It was right about this time that the phone rang. You guessed it—it was my friend, finally, and of course, at the perfect moment. We had a wonderful, healing conversation and I couldn't have felt more different from the awful state I'd been in just hours before. The obstacles that had prevented us from speaking had caused me great pain and the pain had driven me deeper into the truth, causing me to see myself and the situation from a new, more enlightened point of view. I had just experienced exactly what Secret Number Four is about!

Years ago someone shared this saying with me:

Hidden within the poison of our pain is our liberation.

Isn't this a wonderful teaching? It is another way to say that obstacles are lessons in disguise. When you learn to use your pain, your difficulties, your challenges as stepping-stones on your path, you discover the marvelous secret that they do lead you to liberation. *At the end of the tunnel of pain is always more freedom.*

Why Is This Happening to Me?

The basic difference between an ordinary man and a warrior
is that a warrior takes everything as a challenge,
while the ordinary man takes everything as a blessing
or a curse.
CARLOS CASTENADA

Either one of two things is true: *Either everything that is happening in our lives makes sense and is part of a higher purpose, or there's no purpose to anything whatsoever.* At some point in our conscious growth, we need to make a decision about where we stand on this issue. Is there a purpose to life or not? Are we here to grow and learn, or not? Are the difficulties we face acting as teachers and opportunities, or are they simply random events of bad luck?

For me, the decision is simple—I must believe that life is structured on the basis of cosmic principles. I see too much evidence of that all around me. And the alternative, believing that everything is random and chaotic in nature, just doesn't serve my growth from day to day. As the comic genius Woody Allen said, "What if everything is an illusion and nothing exists? In that case, I definitely overpaid for my carpet."

Or to put it more seriously, since everything else that exists in nature has a specific and intelligent purpose, I must believe there is a reason things happen as they happen in my life. It is this understanding that allows me to honor my obstacles.

Honoring your obstacles means knowing they have not been put in your life to make you angry, drive you crazy, or punish you, but that your obstacles are your greatest teachers. Rather than misinterpreting their presence as a sign that you are doing something wrong, begin to recognize these obstacles as an integral and invaluable part of your journey and open yourself to the lessons they offer.

How many times in your life have you been going through a crisis, and found yourself either thinking or saying out loud,

"Why is this happening to me?"

Usually when we ask this question, we aren't expecting an answer. In fact, when we say these words, we often really mean,

"Why are you doing this to me?"

We address our anger to a person, to God, to fate, or whomever we feel is responsible for our suffering.

If we believe the principle behind Secret Number Four, however, that our obstacles are lessons in disguise, then there may actually be an answer to what we thought was a rhetorical question: Why is this happening to me? I believe that those answers are inside of you and that if you look for them, you will find them.

Here is a powerful exercise that I use to discover the hidden lessons in my obstacles:

On the top of a blank piece of paper, write a sentence that describes your obstacle. For instance: "My boyfriend says he's not sure if he wants to make a permanent commitment to me."

Underneath that statement, write the question: "Why is this happening to me?"

Then, close your eyes, take some deep breaths, and ask for guidance and wisdom from whatever higher power you believe in: God, the Divine Mother, cosmic intelligence, etc. Hold the situation in your mind, and just keep asking, "Why is this happening to me?" and then let your mind be still and listen for an answer. At some point, open your eyes, take a pen, and start to write whatever comes out as an answer to that question. Don't judge what you are putting on the paper—just let the words flow without editing them. Continue writing until you feel nothing more is coming out. When you are finished, read back what you have written. You will be amazed at the wisdom and clarity that emerges from that quiet space within you.

It takes a lot of courage to ask yourself, "Why is this happening to me?" You may get responses that are difficult to hear. Maybe you ask, "Why is this happening to me?" about a particular situation and get an answer that says, "You are so used to being in control and this is teaching you patience and surrender," or "You are so arrogant and stubborn that you need something like this to humble you," or "Your heart has been so closed that it took someone leaving you for you to finally feel again," or "You have been so identified with your success that you would never learn to love yourself unconditionally unless you had gone bankrupt." But as painful as it may be to contemplate some of the messages you hear from your inner voice of wisdom, the information you receive will be a great gift.

> When we learn how to look for the true purpose
> in our obstacles,
> we can use them to grow
> and receive the gift they are trying to give us.

There Must Be a Blessing Somewhere

In his book *A Deep Breath of Life*, author and teacher Alan Cohen refers to an experiment some psychologists did on children's attitudes. They filled a room with new toys and then placed a child who was considered negative and ungrateful in the room. He went from one toy to the next very quickly, playing with each for a few moments, then turned to the researcher and complained that he was bored and needed something else to do.

Now it was time for the experiment with the second child. He had been described as very positive and optimistic about everything. So the scientists placed him in a room with a big pile of horse manure. As they watched for his reaction, they were amazed to see a bright smile appear on his face.

"Why are you so happy?" the researcher asked the boy.

"Because there must be a pony somewhere!" he responded happily.

I have thought about this story so often since I first read it. Each time I find myself in a situation that feels like a room with a pile of manure, or each time it seems like someone has dumped a pile of manure at my doorstep, I try to say to myself, **"There must be a blessing somewhere."** And I keep my eyes and heart open for it.

Sometimes, though, all you can see is the pile of manure and you haven't found the pony yet. Sometimes, no matter how much you try to recognize the higher purpose of a problem, you just can't do it. Something painful is happening to you and in spite of all of your attempts to look for the lesson, none can be found. These kinds of obstacles are the most challenging of all, for they tempt you to feel persecuted by life, punished by what is happening to you, and filled with hopelessness.

Just because you can't see the lesson doesn't mean it's not there. It is. But it may take time to reveal itself. That's where your understanding and your faith comes in. You need to keep going forward, to do your best at dealing with the issues confronting you and trust that there is a blessing somewhere, and that when the time is right, it will reveal itself.

A few weeks ago I was driving from Northern California back home to Southern California. It was nighttime and I suddenly entered an area of the state known for its dense fog. Within seconds, I couldn't see a foot past the front of my car. The road before me seemed to have totally disappeared and I was surrounded by a thick, white mist. I slowed down to a crawl and fixed my gaze on the tiny piece of highway that I could see. That's how I drove for almost two hours.

As I inched my way along, I thought about how many times in my life I'd felt this same way, as if all at once a thick, impenetrable fog had descended over me and I lost all my sense of direction. I didn't know where I was, I didn't know where I was going, or even if I'd get there safely. Every day, every hour seemed to take forever and I didn't feel I was making any progress at all.

Then, sometimes just as suddenly, the fog would lift, the obstacles would vanish, and I would find myself in a much stronger, happier place than I could have ever imagined. "How did I get here?" I would wonder, for it hadn't seemed like I was really advancing at all. And yet, I had been and I would look back and appreciate the journey with new understanding.

And this is just what happened to me that night as I drove. Suddenly, just like that, the fog was gone. It didn't slowly fade away—I just finally reached the spot where it didn't exist anymore. One moment I couldn't see a thing and the next, everything was clear and I found myself looking out at the beautiful California mountains illuminated by a crescent moon, gazing in the distance at the twinkling lights of civilization.

When we are driving on a highway and we get hit with fog, we know that eventually we will arrive at our destination. But in life, when we get fogged in by difficulties and obstacles, we often fear we will get lost and never make it home. Remember—the road *is* there in front of you, even if you can't see it. *The road isn't lost, and no matter how frightened you feel, neither are you. You're exactly where you need to be.* Just keep going, and soon you'll be in the clear once more.

Learning to Honor Your Obstacles

Secret Number Four suggests that you honor your obstacles. When you read that, did you think, "Well, I can see accepting my obstacles, even learning something from them, but *honoring* them? No way"? We think of honoring circumstances and people we love and for whom we are grateful. So it may, indeed, seem odd, if not impossible, to honor your pain, your problems, your difficulties. *How can you honor something that seems to be making you so miserable?*

I certainly sympathize with this point of view. I have spent most of my life in a battle with my obstacles. Whenever one would appear, I would immediately begin to strategize: How quickly could I get rid of this awful situation? What could I do to control it, manipulate it, outsmart it, outmaneuver it? I believed that the purpose of that obstacle being in my life was for me to fight against it and win and that if it went away, I would be victorious.

The problem with this thinking is that it only makes things worse. Why? Because:

> Obstacles are not enemies to be eliminated,
> but friends in disguise,
> who come bearing offerings of wisdom
> and understanding.
> When you treat these gift-bearers as robbers,
> you miss out on the treasures they are trying
> to deliver.

Imagine that someone told you a great saint and teacher was going to arrive at your home on a particular evening to offer you blessings and spiritual initiation. How would you greet her? Would you open the door just a crack and shout, "Go away! I can't believe you showed up here! Why does this always happen to me?" Would you take a frying pan and hit her over the head, hoping to knock her unconscious so you wouldn't have to deal with her? Would you invite her in, but look at your watch every five seconds, wondering to yourself, "When is this nightmare going to be over?" Would you turn up your stereo as loud as possible and stick your fingers in your ears so you wouldn't have to listen to anything she was trying to tell you?

Of course you would do no such things. If you knew a great saint was coming to visit you, you would run around making preparations so that everything looked beautiful. When she arrived, you would welcome her into your home with great love. You would listen intently to the words she spoke, knowing they contained invaluable wisdom and guidance. And when it was time for her to leave, you would thank her with all your heart for coming and bringing you such blessings. *In other words, you would honor her.*

In the dictionary, one of the definitions of the word *honor* is "to treat with respect and reverence." This is the first step in learning to honor your obstacles—**to stop treating them as if they are evil-doers sent by your worst enemy and begin treating them with respect and reverence, as if they are gift-bearers sent by your most caring guides and angels . . . because they are!**

You may think, "Well, this is a lovely analogy, but how can I not wish that a painful situation would go away? How can I not wish that a crisis would end?" And of course, you're right. It's natural to want to be free of suffering. But remember—obstacles are very purposeful. They have something specific to deliver to you. The longer you take to receive the message, the longer they will stick around!

**Obstacles won't dissolve
until they teach you what they came to teach you.**

What if a messenger has been instructed to come to your home and read you a telegram containing some important information, and you are so busy beating him over the head with pots and pans to try and scare him away that you can't hear what he is attempting to tell you? He'll just keep standing there until you're ready to listen. He has nowhere else to go.

This is a sobering thought, but one that can be motivating, as well. If there are lessons you are meant to learn through your obstacles, do you want to take five years to learn them, or five days? Do you want to struggle and resist, or do you want to work toward getting the message as quickly as possible, so that the messenger will be on his way?

Getting What I Asked For

Sometimes, when those messengers come knocking on our door, we forget that we're actually the ones who invited them in the first place!

"What are you doing here?" we say rudely, when the obstacle shows up.

"Isn't this Barbara's house?"

"Yeah, so who are you?"

"I'm a cosmic messenger, bringing you your latest important lesson disguised in the form of this crisis."

"I didn't order any lessons," we shout as we try to push the messenger out of the doorway, "so just take your crisis and give it to somebody else!"

"Oh, but you're mistaken, my dear," the messenger calmly replies, walking past us into the center of the living room. "Why, just last week, didn't you pray to become stronger and more content within yourself? How fortunate for you that you get such a quick response to your requests. Very impressive, really. Now, where shall I put this pile of difficulty that you ordered?"

We usually don't remember inviting obstacles into
our life,
but if we have ever prayed for growth,
for happiness, for freedom,
then we've opened ourselves up to receiving
the lessons
necessary to create those higher states of
consciousness.

A few years ago, I experienced a profound reminder of the power of inviting growth into my life. I had just spent many months focusing my energies solely on my spiritual growth. I meditated, I chanted, I prayed, I studied. I felt very centered, very peaceful, and heartened that finally, everything seemed to be calm and in place.

Suddenly, and seemingly out of nowhere, an enormous crisis erupted in my personal life. I was shocked—how could this be? Everything had been going so well. And in spite of everything I knew about the futility of resisting obstacles, I actually found myself thinking, "I want this to go away!"

I began calling every kind of spiritual guide I knew, astrologers, psychics, asking them, "When will this be over? When will it end?" They all agreed—a big shift was coming. "Great," I thought with relief. And they were right. Things did shift—they got much worse!

Each day, I would sit in meditation and feel so much anger. Who was I angry at? I knew the answer: *Secretly, I was angry at God.* After all, I had just spent the last few years immersed in all kinds of spiritual practices, praying for true freedom, releasing my attachment to the kinds of outer accomplishments I used to believe would make me happy, and this is how I was getting repaid for my efforts? And naturally, the more angry I felt, the more disconnected I became from that source of peace and love inside me which *is* God, and the more unhappy I became.

Thank God for grace. Because one day as I went through my usual routine in meditation of crying and wondering how this crisis could be happening to me, I suddenly felt the presence of a beautiful being of love and light in a female form standing before me. I instinctively knew that she represented God, spirit in its form as a teacher. She said to me very clearly, **"Haven't you been praying for liberation? Haven't you been praying for oneness and unconditional love? Haven't you been praying to really ascend in this life? Did you think I didn't** hear you? I heard you. Did you think I didn't answer? **THIS IS THE ANSWER.**"

The impact of these words literally knocked me over from the position I'd been sitting in on the floor. All at once, everything became perfectly clear. For the past few years, I *had* been praying intensely, fervently for liberation, for oneness, for the ultimate growth. I *had* been praying for a dramatic breakthrough in my consciousness. But I held a spiritually immature concept of what that breakthrough would look like—my life was supposed to just get easier and easier until one day I was supremely happy, no more problems, no more obstacles ever again.

But that's not how it works. Rebirth, like birth itself, is messy. It's bloody. It's painful. And out of that pain emerges the miracle of new life. That's what was happening to me. I was being pushed through the birth canal, and I was angrily screaming and kicking and shouting, "Why are you doing this terrible thing to me?" and God was smiling and saying, "Why, I'm just answering your prayers!"

The moment I heard what that voice said to me in meditation, I knew that it was true. What I had been looking at as a curse, as my bad karma, as unfavorable astrological signs, as somebody else's psychological problems ruining my life, all these were powerful lessons and gifts in disguise. I had been angry at God for "ruining things," when in fact, God was giving me exactly what I had asked for.

I came out of that meditation a very different woman

from who I was when I went in. I had, indeed, invited the universe to take me higher, to free me, and it was responding. What had I expected that kind of life-changing transformation to look like—a few rough days, a few small revelations about myself? No, big lessons require big events to get them across.

Standing where I am in my life now, and looking back on that time, I am still astonished to see how masterfully it forced me to go through exactly the experiences I needed in order to make enormous personal breakthroughs. I am so grateful for the obstacles I had to face and I am especially grateful for the very strong but loving message I received in that meditation. I'd needed to be reminded that my soul was getting exactly what it had prayed for, no matter how impossible this seemed, and that the messenger at my door was delivering what would turn out to be a great blessing.

Please understand that I'm not saying we get exactly what we ask for down to the detail. Of course, I hadn't actually prayed for that specific crisis. And even after that inspiring experience, I still wasn't particularly thrilled with the disguises in which the lessons had dressed themselves up. That's only natural. None of us actually prays for the unpleasant specifics of how we want to learn and grow. For instance, I doubt that you have ever prayed, "Please God, I want to be fired from my job and be out of work for months," or, "Please God, let my landlord say I have to move out of my house with no warning" or, "Please God, make my husband have an affair."

But the universe will do whatever it takes and use

whatever it can to get us to grow. Therefore, we need to give it creative license in terms of *how* it processes us. Here's a hint—it will use everything you've got lying around in your life, your relationships, your career, your family members, your possessions, your body—whatever you're attached to and care about to teach you what you need to learn.

Honoring Your Obstacles Doesn't Mean You Have to Like Them

Here's another reminder about honoring your obstacles:

It's okay to know something good is happening to you and still not like the way it feels.

I think this is where some of us get confused, thinking that if we honor our obstacles and the lessons they are teaching us, we shouldn't be uncomfortable while the process is taking place. That would be impossible. Remember, we've talked about how growth and change are usually *very* uncomfortable and the bigger the lessons, the more discomfort we can expect. So I'm not suggesting you walk around trying to convince yourself, "I'm having a wonderful time getting divorced because I know I am learning important lessons." It won't work. But you can hold this understanding in your awareness:

> "What's happening to me *feels* bad,
> but I know good is going to come out of it."

You can take this one step further and replace the word *bad* with the word *uncomfortable* or the word *challenging*. We discussed this in earlier chapters, but I'll remind you again that just because something is uncomfortable or even painful does *not* necessarily mean it is bad for you. And when we're talking about obstacles and the lessons they offer, we know that what feels "bad" is, indeed, going to be very good for us in the long run.

So imagine saying the following as a way of honoring your obstacles:

> "Today was really an *uncomfortable* day."
> "My husband and I had a *challenging* conversation."
> "I am going through a *challenging* time."
> "I have a very *uncomfortable* relationship with my mother."
> "I am having a *challenging* hair day!"

Honoring your obstacles also doesn't necessarily mean honoring the person or situation who is part of that obstacle. For instance:

I have a good friend who discovered that a man she was dating had been lying to her from the beginning of the relationship about many things, including the fact that she was not the only woman he was sleeping with!

Naturally, she felt hurt, betrayed, and furious. We spent many hours discussing her plight, and I supported her in getting past her anger at this man and trying to find the lessons in the situation for herself. And with a little bit of effort she found them, and learned a lot about how, in her eagerness to love and connect in relationships, she often projects qualities onto men that she wishes they would have, whether they have them or not!

One day, many months after her heartbreak, she called me and said she was very confused about something and wanted my advice. "I want to really honor that painful experience with Bruce (not his real name)," she began, "and to feel complete with it. *But I am afraid if I feel grateful that it happened, and see it as a wonderful part of my growth, I will somehow be condoning his terrible behavior, and saying it was O.K.*"

I understood my friend's dilemma perfectly. She felt that to honor her obstacle, she would somehow be honoring Bruce, and she didn't want to honor Bruce because she felt Bruce had been a very bad boy!

"Honoring your obstacle means understanding the higher purpose it served in your life," I explained. "It means extracting the lesson from it. **It means being grateful for the experience.** But you don't have to be personally grateful to Bruce!"

Needless to say, my friend was very relieved. She felt she had already given up a lot of her power to Bruce and was concerned that by honoring her obstacle and relinquishing her resentment, she would be somehow taking a position of weakness. But when we find the gift in our difficulties, we will always become empowered.

Resentment toward our obstacles never empowers us.
Our true power comes from our ability
to find the lessons and gifts
in every difficult experience
and be grateful for them.

What to Do When You Encounter Obstacles in Your Life

When you are pushed, pull.
When you are pulled, push.
Find the natural course and bend with it,
then you join with nature's power.
DAN MILLMAN

Have you ever sat on the banks of a rushing stream and watched the water flow by? If you look carefully, you will see that the stream contains many obstacles to the path of the water. There are rocks, boulders, tree trunks, all in the way. But what does the water do? *It just flows.*

Suppose there is a huge boulder in the path of the river. Does the water stay in a straight line as it's stubbornly hitting the boulder over and over and over again, like water from a hose that refuses to change direction? No, it just flows around the boulder. It divides itself, it finds new passageways, it goes up on the riverbanks if it has to—it does anything it can do to get around that obstacle. It goes with the flow.

For some reason, when we hit obstacles we have this thought that if we push even harder against them, we'll get through them. But that's not what Nature teaches us. *It teaches us to yield, to adjust, to try a different route.*

We talked a little bit about learning to flow with change in chapter three and the same philosophy applies to dealing with your obstacles. So you can begin by honoring the presence of that boulder, that obstacle, rather than pretending it doesn't exist. Then, instead of taking an aggressive stand against a problem or a challenge and thinking, "I am going to annihilate you. I am going to blast you out of my life," start by just letting go, and seeing if perhaps there isn't another way around the issue you hadn't seen before. The way we are forced to deal with our problems is always the direction the universe is trying to steer us in anyway. And it always turns out for the best, even if we can't see it at the time.

Like the water in a stream, soften yourself
and go around the corners of your obstacles.
There, right before your eyes, will be new directions
and new wisdom just waiting to be discovered.

Another way to flow more and resist less is to watch how you pray and ask for help. Your first impulse will be what mine has always been: "Please God, remove this obstacle. Please make it go away. Please get rid of this situation." Now, if you are going to put the principle behind Secret Number Four into practice, you already know that a prayer like this isn't going to get much of a response. After all, your obstacles are not enemies you want God to help you vanquish—indeed, they are gifts and opportunities *from* God. So asking God to remove them may not go over really well.

I'm going to suggest that you do something different:

> If you pray about your problems, pray to have the
>   wisdom to discover the gift in your obstacles.
> Pray to be able to receive what's being offered to
>   you.
> Pray to have the courage to be honest with
>   yourself and see what the obstacle is trying to
>   teach you about your soul.
> Pray to learn how to honor your obstacles.

Try this. It will bring you amazing results.

Earlier I suggested that you do a writing exercise asking yourself, "Why is this happening to me?" in order to uncover some of the lessons hidden within your obstacles. Here are some more questions that you can use in meditation, or in journal writing, or in sharing with a friend that can reveal your own great inner wisdom that already has the answers you are looking for:

Questions To Ask Yourself
When Confronted with an Obstacle

How am I falling apart in a way that is beneficial?

What is this crisis revealing about me to me?

If God was choosing this for me, what was he/she thinking?

Why might this be necessary in my life right now?

How can I go through this gracefully and consciously?

How can I use this to grow?

What is God trying to teach me?

The Perfect Problems Lead to the Perfect Freedom

I began this chapter with a quote by a great Indian saint: "The perfect problems lead to the perfect freedom." This is a powerful contemplation. To think of your problems, your obstacles as perfect, to have faith that they will lead you to the freedom you seek—these ideas can radically transform your experience of life.

There is a classic metaphor that has been used in spiritual teachings around the world for the way in which God and the universe works on us. It is the image of a potter and his clay. The potter has a vision of a beautiful clay pot he wants to create. So first, he takes the clay and pounds it and pounds it to get all the air out. Then, he places the lump of clay on his potter's wheel and as the wheel turns, the potter begins to mold it into the shape he wants.

Now, as the clay hardens, the potter begins to strike at the pot, beating it into shape. If you only watched the hand that was beating at the pot from all sides, you might think the potter was being cruel and careless, even trying to destroy his own creation. But if you looked more closely, you would notice that the potter's other hand was deep inside of the pot, supporting it so it could withstand the blows that were making it strong and beautiful, supporting it so that it would not collapse under his expert efforts to mold it into the perfect shape.

Both of the potter's hands are doing what they do with love. The hand that strikes the blows at the outside of the pot does so because it loves the clay and wants to turn it into something beautiful. And the hand that supports the inside of the pot does so because it loves the clay and does not want it to crack.

Think of yourself as a mound of clay that God is molding into an exquisite work of art unlike any other. Yes, you feel the hard blows, removing this piece, polishing that one, reshaping and reforming you over and over again. But feel, too, that hand of compassion, that hand of protection always supporting you from within, holding you up when you think you will fall, giving you strength when you are sure you will break apart. That is the hand of grace; that is the hand of God.

You are being turned into something so very beautiful.

Your Mind Creates Your Experience of Reality, So Learn to Make Your Mind Your Friend

We either make ourselves miserable,
or we make ourselves strong.
The amount of work is the same.

CARLOS CASTENADA

Did you know that you possess an extraordinary and magical power? It is the power to make yourself feel happy or sad in an instant. It is the power to create chaos or confusion where it doesn't exist or to see perfection and wonder in whatever is before you. This power affects everyone with whom you come in contact, either repelling them or attracting them. It can make you appear beautiful or unappealing, lovable or aloof, charismatic and confident, or frightened and insecure. It can be an unending source of inspiration and creativity or a malevolent force that sabotages your success and undermines your dreams.

What is the amazing power that can do all of these things?

It is the power of your own mind.

We spend our lives seeking out those things that will give us a sense of power, a feeling that we can control our lives. But we already possess the greatest power we could ever want. In fact, whether we know it or not, we're using this power every day to shape our destinies. The problem is that, like a sorceress in training who doesn't yet comprehend or appreciate the mysterious potency of her magic wand, we still haven't learned the secrets of the amazing power of our minds. How does this magical instrument of your mind work?

Your mind works through the power of projection.

Think about the last time you went to the movies. You sat in the theater and watched a drama unfold on the screen before you. You saw people laugh, cry, fight, make love, and you felt moved in very real ways. But none of that was *actually* taking place on the screen, was it? The actors weren't a part of the screen; the buildings weren't a part of the screen. They were being *projected* onto the screen by a film projector. And in spite of how real it all seemed, you knew it was just an illusion.

This is exactly how your mind works. You have the equivalent of a blank "screen"—it is called your consciousness, or awareness. It is neutral, just like the movie screen, holding no images of its own. *Your mind is like the film projector, projecting images and stories onto your screen of consciousness.* These images and stories become the movie of your life. They become your moment-by-moment experience. They become what you call your "reality."

If your mind is the projector of reality, then what is the film? It is your stored-up emotional impressions, experiences, wounds, and issues you've carried around since childhood and if you believe in reincarnation, even from other lives. This film is a collection of unresolved feelings that gets projected onto people and situations that you encounter day by day.

The problem is that we often forget we're watching a movie projected by our mind and begin to think what we are seeing is very real. It would be as if you were watching a film and got so involved in what was on the screen that you stood up in the theater and started shouting to the characters: "Watch out! There's someone behind you," or "Don't you see that he's cheating on you? For God's sake, leave him while you still have some self-respect left," or "I hate men like you—you're despicable!"

This is what your mind does. It doesn't just *observe* reality and give you an objective report of what is happening. Instead, it *projects* your own, unconscious internal reality onto people and situations, like a film projector projects an image onto the screen. And if some of your internal reality is made up of unpleasant emotions such as fear, worry, sadness, anger, feelings of being unloved—just to name a few—your mind may project these emotions and reactions onto situations where they really don't exist.

> So much of what appears to be real in our lives
> is just a projection of a less-than-clear mind.

Here's an example of how your mind uses projection to create reality: Let's say you spent an evening with a new friend, during which you had some very honest conversations about both of your lives. You felt vulnerable opening up this much, but happy that it seemed you were becoming close to this person. The next day, you leave a message on her answering machine, thanking her for the great time and asking her to give you a call back.

Several days pass and you don't hear from this woman. Your mind takes this information and adds its own projection to form some conclusions. *"Maybe she's mad at me,"* you begin to worry. *"Maybe she thought I was too open. Maybe I said something to offend her. I hate this—this always happens when I'm honest with people. It turns them off."* Another few days pass and your concerns escalate, and your mind adds even more to the pot of worries: *"What if I've scared her off for good, and just when we were getting so close? She's probably hoping she never hears from me again. I just can't trust other women."*

Now five days have gone by, still no phone call and your mind projects more and more drama onto the situation: *"There's no doubt anymore—she's obviously angry with me. Should I call and apologize? What if she says horrible things to me on the phone? No, I'd better wait for her to call me. Come to think of it, I haven't heard from another girlfriend for a while, the one who introduced me to this new friend. Maybe they've been talking about me. Maybe everyone's gossiping about me."* Your stomach is in knots, you can't concentrate on your work, and you're a mess.

That night, as you're sitting in your room feeling panicky and sorry for yourself, the phone rings. It's your friend! "I'm so sorry I didn't call you back sooner," she apologizes in a warm voice. "I was called out of town suddenly by my company and have been in nonstop meetings on a big project for days. We barely got time to eat. Anyway, it's finally over, and I just got back this afternoon. By the way, I had a wonderful time the other night, and I'm so glad we are building a close friendship."

Gulp. . . . What about the rejection, the drama, the betrayal? It doesn't exist and it never did. But you just spent a week in hell—where did that hell come from? It came from your own mind.

What *actually* happened to you during that week? I don't mean what you *thought* was happening, but what *actually* happened? The answer is: NOTHING AT ALL. Nothing actually happened. All the action took place in your mind. Your mind created a reality in which you were rejected, betrayed, conspired against. It felt real, but it wasn't real.

Doesn't this sound familiar? This same scenario happens to you and me and all of us dozens of times every day, hundreds of times a week, thousands of times a month, tens of thousands of times every year, and millions of times over the course of our lives. Your mind writes the script for what it believes is going on and you read your lines and act the part, often without questioning whether or not you even want to play that particular role!

> Most of your experience of life takes place in
> your mind.
> What you experience as real is very dependent upon
> what you *think* is real.

Isn't this an amazing insight? This means that our experience of reality is *subjective*. So for instance, if I *think* you are angry with me, I will actually have the experience that you are angry with me. If I *think* people are feeling uncomfortable around me, I will actually have the experience that people are uncomfortable around me. *Whatever I think, I will experience as real,* and to the extent that my thoughts are powerful, my experience will be that much more real.

This is a radical idea, because most of us think that reality is a hard, solid entity, when in truth it is very soft, very pliable, very subjective. One obvious example of this is time. You would probably say that since time is measurable, it has a certain definite reality. But the great scientist and philosopher Albert Einstein introduced the world to the Theory of Relativity, which explains that time, along with many other supposedly definable, objective realities, is very relative, very subjective. Here's what Einstein said once in explaining this theory to his students: "A day spent with a beautiful woman seems like a moment; an hour at a job you hate feels like an eternity." So what determines how you experience that day or that hour? Your mind. When you are happy, time appears to go so quickly. When you are unhappy, time drags and seems to almost stand still. But in each case, the amount of minutes is the same, isn't it? *It's your consciousness, your mind that's different.*

How Your Thoughts Create Reality

Not only do your mind's projections affect your reality, but they affect other people's, as well. In fact, what your mind projects and worries about can actually become true, even if it wasn't true in the first place.

I recall a very vivid experience of this power of the mind to affect others. Years ago, I was working on a creative project and knew I would be collaborating with a man I'd never met. I asked a colleague if she knew anything about this person and she rolled her eyes. "He's awful!" she began. "My assistant worked with him a few years ago on a show and said it was the worst experience of her life. I've heard he is arrogant, mean, and makes everyone around him miserable. And he especially dislikes strong women."

"Oh, boy," I thought to myself, "I'm in trouble."

For the next few weeks, I couldn't stop worrying about this man and the dreaded meeting that was coming up shortly. "How am I going to handle someone so difficult?" I wondered. The closer I got to the first day of working together, the more anxious and tense I became.

Finally, the moment arrived. I was barely breathing as I walked into the conference room and was introduced to the person I'd heard so much about. I stared at him intensely as we shook hands, noticing how expressionless his face was, and I thought, "It's true, he has no heart at all. He's seems to be so cold."

Things went downhill from there. I was so wary of everything he said and was just waiting for him to make a caustic comment. At one point, he complimented someone else on a job he'd done, and I thought, "Boy, that was insincere—what a token thing to say." As the meeting progressed, the tension mounted—until you could just about cut it with a knife.

I drove home that evening wondering how I would get through the next few weeks. This guy was a nightmare! He'd been uptight and on edge the whole day. I'd never been so uncomfortable in a professional situation before.

The next morning, to my horror, this man asked if he could speak with me alone. "Oh, my God," I thought, "Here's where he's going to launch into me."

"Barbara," he began in a low voice, "is something bothering you?"

"Why?" I answered defensively, waiting for the ax to fall.

"Well, I got the distinct impression yesterday that you didn't like me," he said softly, "and it was a real disappointment, because I've been looking forward to working with you for a while now."

What was this? He sounded different, almost . . . nice.

"Actually," I said taking a deep breath, "I thought *you* didn't like *me* from the minute I walked into the room. You seemed so tense."

The man laughed. "That's because I was nervous meeting you. I've heard so much about you and your work, and wanted you to feel I was the right person for this project."

Could I be hearing him correctly? Him, nervous about meeting me? I swallowed and said, "Why didn't you think I liked you?"

"Well, you hardly looked at me when I shook your hand, you didn't smile once the whole day, and to be honest, you seemed really tense. I figured either you weren't happy with the producer's choice of me, or you were just a cold person."

I could hardly believe my ears. His impression of me was the same as my impression of him. Suddenly, I saw exactly what had been happening. I'd walked into that meeting radiating enormous anxiety and dislike after weeks of projecting all kinds of negative impressions onto this man. I was just waiting for him to make one false move and I'd have the evidence that my mind was correct in its assumptions. He picked up on my attitude instantly and became equally tense, thus fulfilling all my worst expectations. The more tense and suspicious I was, the more tense he was and within moments he did, indeed, appear to be as objectionable as I had anticipated. But I was the one who was causing him to be objectionable. *He was reacting to what I projected, and fulfilled my negative expectations to a tee.* I had created the reality my mind had worried about.

There was nothing else to do but tell this man the truth, and that's just what I did. He didn't remember the woman who'd said he was so difficult, but did share with me that he'd been going through a very painful divorce at the time and probably wasn't the easiest guy to be around. I apologized for walking into the meeting with such preconceived notions about him and found as we talked that I liked him very much. I was so grateful that he'd spoken up. If he hadn't, we would have both continued to think the other person was horrible and would have created a very different reality from the one we were designing in the moment.

The project turned out to be one of the most enjoyable working experiences of my career. And it taught me a huge lesson about the power my mind has, not only to create my internal, subjective reality, but to affect the external, objective reality, as well.

**Your mind will always look for evidence
to prove that it's right.**

Have you noticed this about your mind? If you believe something, you look for evidence to support that belief, to the exclusion of anything else. I didn't pay attention to anything good about that man during our first meeting. In fact, I invalidated any positive qualities as insincere and instead, my mind prowled around for whatever it could find to prove its case. I wasn't open to seeing the reality at hand. I was intent on corroborating the reality in my mind!

Imagine how often you and I allow our mind's negative expectations to determine our fate and rob us of the wonderful possibility that awaits us in each moment.

Here's the fifth principle:

SECRET NUMBER FIVE:

**YOUR MIND CREATES YOUR
EXPERIENCE OF REALITY,
SO LEARN TO MAKE YOUR
MIND YOUR FRIEND**

This is an ancient truth that has been written about in so many of the world's greatest scriptures from both eastern and western cultures, dating back thousands of years.

> *Thought is creative.*
> *The world is as you see it.*
> *As you think, so you are.*

Your mind is infinitely powerful. From moment to moment, it creates your reality by how it reacts, interprets, or projects. Left to its own devices, your mind can cause you great suffering or great contentment; it can imprison you, or free you. An uncontrolled mind can turn a neutral moment into a painful moment. It can turn nothing into something. It can create misery where there wasn't any.

Would you let a wild animal loose in your house, allowing it to tear up your furniture and destroy your belongings? Would you let an unsupervised child run through the rooms screaming, knocking things over, and interrupting your work or tasks? Of course not. And yet, most of us let our minds run wild in our lives like a untamed animal or a child having a tantrum, creating havoc, stealing our inner peace, and causing every possible kind of trouble.

Secret Number Five says that since your mind creates your experience of reality, you need to learn to make your mind your friend. You've seen how powerful your mind is. Making your mind your friend means learning to use that power in a *constructive* way rather than a *destructive* way.

> Your mind uses just as much of its power
> to make you unhappy and unfulfilled
> as it would to make you happy and fulfilled.
> The task becomes learning to make your mind
> work *for* you
> and not *against* you.

As the mystical author Carlos Castenada says at the beginning of this chapter, "We either make ourselves miserable, or we make ourselves strong. The amount of work is the same." Understanding this principle and learning tools for mastering the habits of the mind can radically change your day-to-day experience of people and circumstances and put you in charge of your moods and your happiness. There are two steps to learning to make your mind your friend that I'll be sharing with you in the rest of this chapter:

1. Becoming aware of what your mind is doing.
2. Making a choice to do something different that is more beneficial to you.

How Your Mind Can Be Your Greatest Enemy

None of us likes to have enemies. None of us likes to feel someone is trying to undermine our happiness. Yet there are times in our lives when we wonder: *"Who's out to get me? Who's hurting me? Who's not loving me? Who's not supporting me?"* Naturally, we try to stay away from people who want to harm us, and avoid situations in which we are being undermined.

Do you know who your greatest enemy in the world is? **It is your own mind.** As difficult as this may be to believe, it is true. And one of the first steps in turning your mind into a friend is becoming more aware of how, when you don't pay attention, it can act as your enemy.

"Enemy is a strong word," you may be thinking to yourself. "Maybe my mind gets out of control sometimes, but my enemy? That's hard to comprehend." Let me show you what I mean.

Imagine a typical morning in your life, getting ready for your day. You've just taken a shower and you step out to dry yourself. As you do, you look in the mirror and perhaps something like this goes on in your mind:

"Look at you! I can't believe how much your stomach is sticking out. You look pregnant, for God's sake. And look at that cellulite all over your thighs, how gross! Oh, your body makes me sick. Well, I'm not surprised—you have been eating like a pig lately, stuffing your face late at night. You just have no discipline at all. And what's this? Ugh, sagging skin on your face. So ugly! You look awful."

You finish drying yourself off, and go about your day, thinking nothing of what just happened before the mirror.

Now, imagine this same scene, but with a different twist: Let's say that you are married and as you step out of the shower one morning, your husband walks into the bathroom, looks you up and down, and says: *"Look at you! I can't believe how much your stomach is sticking out. You look pregnant, for God's sake. And look at that cellulite all over your thighs, how gross! Oh, your body makes me sick. Well, I'm not surprised—you have been eating like a pig lately, stuffing your face late at night. You just have no discipline at all. And what's this? Ugh, sagging skin on your face. So ugly! You look awful."*

How would you react if your mate talked to you this way? You'd be furious. You'd be enraged. You'd feel like slapping his face. "How dare you speak to me that way!" you'd say in a horrified voice. What if you heard someone addressing one of your friends or children this way? Would you stand silently by and watch? Of course not. You'd intervene and say, "I refuse to allow you to abuse this person."

Yet perhaps this is how you talk to yourself all the time—and that was just the first thirty seconds of the day! Add to that what your mind does as you deal with your kids or go to work or try to get everything done you are supposed to, and imagine how many negative comments it makes about you in a twenty-four-hour period.

If you really want to get a spiritual wake-up call, try this experiment:

For just one day, make an agreement with yourself that you will do your best to be aware of your thoughts and you'll write down every single negative thought that your mind has. Carry a little notebook with you and each time you notice your mind having an unsupportive thought, write it down. For instance:

"You look so fat in this outfit."
"That was a really stupid thing to say."
"You'll never close this deal."
"I can't believe you forgot to pick up the clothes at the cleaners."

At the end of the day, count how many negative thoughts you've listed about yourself, and I guarantee that you will be shocked at the amount. And I also guarantee you, no one will have had more critical thoughts about you that day than *you*.

This is negative self-talk, the way we let our mind mistreat us. We give it free reign to change our mood, influence our behavior, and determine our state of well-being. Isn't it ironic that we work so hard in life to be comfortable, to avoid being with people who make us uncomfortable, to avoid being in places that make us uncomfortable, and yet our own minds are the source of our greatest discomfort?

When you allow your mind to be your enemy
by tolerating its negative self-talk,
you aren't being your own friend.

In each moment, you have a choice—to use your mind to be your friend, or your enemy.

Choosing What You Think

Imagine a restaurant where customers weren't allowed to order their own food and you had to eat whatever the waiter brought you, regardless of whether you liked it or not. And not only that, you had to keep eating as long as food was placed before you even when you weren't hungry anymore. How often do you think you'd go to this place? Probably never! Why? Because you want to choose what you eat.

Well, this is the way it is with our minds. Your mind starts thinking on a certain track and you just go along with it in whatever direction it wants to take you, "eating" whatever thoughts it puts in front of you, regardless of whether you like it or not.

You know how this works, because it happens to you dozens of times a day. You are feeling fine, taking a walk or making dinner or driving somewhere, and suddenly, your mind starts: *"You know, your husband was awfully quiet this morning at breakfast. Maybe something is wrong. After all, it has been three weeks since you've made love. I wonder if he's feeling turned off to you lately. Remember last week when you noticed him staring at that woman at the party? Maybe he's interested in someone else."*

Suddenly, you are anxious and worried, and instead

of enjoying your walk or drive, you're worrying about your relationship, which you know deep inside is fine. It's as if your mind offered you a plate of food labeled: PARANOID THOUGHTS ABOUT GETTING REJECTED BY SOMEONE YOU LOVE, and you reached for it saying, "Mmmmmmm, yum yum, just what I wanted to eat right about now."

Where did that thought come from? *It came from the kitchen of your mind, always cooking up ways to try and deal with its leftover emotions.* This is the way we get yanked around by our thoughts all the time, pushed into places we don't want to go and pulled off track from where we do want to go. *Why* particular thoughts and feelings arise is a question that I've answered in other books, but here the issue is *what* you're going to do about it.

One of the most important changes you can make in your life is to begin choosing what you think about, rather than allowing your mind to determine what you think about.

> **Choose your thoughts**
> **instead of letting your thoughts choose you.**

Every day of your life, you make hundreds of choices. When you get dressed in the morning, you look carefully at your wardrobe and choose what you would like to wear—you don't just bump into a hanger and decide that's your outfit. When you go to the supermarket, you look carefully at the items on the shelves and choose what you need—you don't buy everything you see. *In this same way, you don't have to buy into every thought your mind presents to you.* You can choose to go in the direction thoughts take you, or you can choose to say, "No thank you, I'm not interested in going there right now."

You don't have to pay attention to every thought that comes into your mind.

This is one of the reasons we often feel overwhelmed— we're letting every one of our thoughts take us for a ride without questioning whether we want to go with it or not. It would be as if each time a car passed your house, you ran out and jumped into the backseat and went wherever the driver was going! Then, you'd find your way back to your house and start all over again.

When you notice your mind going in a particular direction, ask yourself:

"Do I want to ride with this thought or not?"

Where is this thought going to take me? To joy, to misery, to empowerment, to fear, to separation, to love? Do I want to go there?

If you decide that a thought is offering you a ride to a destination you aren't interested in, simply replace it with another, more positive, supportive thought. Choose another vehicle for your consciousness.

Practicing Selective Attention

Do you know how strong your mind is? It can focus on one thing to the exclusion of all others for hours and hours. The problem is that it usually focuses on what is *not* helpful and supportive, rather than on what is positive. I call this *selective attention*, the tendency of the mind to zoom in and fixate on something that is bothering it. There's nothing wrong with paying attention to our issues or challenges. But the mind tends to do this to the exclusion of any other thoughts and focus turns into obsession. "I just can't stop thinking about it," you hear yourself saying.

Selective attention is one of the ways our mind can be an enemy, rather than a friend. I used to experience this tendency all the time when I first began my public speaking career. I'd get in front of an audience of perhaps a few hundred people and begin to give a talk. For the first few moments, I'd be calm, confident, and clear. But suddenly, a strange thing would happen: I'd notice my mind scanning the crowd to see who was *not* enjoying my speech. I'd pass over all the smiling faces, the people nodding in agreement, until I found the one person who was sitting there with his arms crossed and no expression on his face. Then, my mind would start its own speech to me: "*Look at him—he is totally bored. You aren't getting through to him at all. Maybe you picked the wrong topic. If you were talking more about sex, I bet people would be having a better time. I wonder if the promoter is disap-*

pointed. See, you just made a joke, and this guy didn't even smile. He thinks he wasted his money."

There could be hundreds of other people in the room hanging onto every word I said, but my mind would give its selective attention to where it had discovered a problem. You can imagine how distracting this was to me. By the time I'd finish my presentation, I would be depressed and feel like a failure. I'd walk off the stage and when the promoter would approach me, I'd apologize for not giving a better talk. "What do you mean?" they'd always say, "You were wonderful." And I'd think to myself, *"The man in the tenth row on the aisle didn't think so. . . ."*

This went on for the first few years of my career. Then one day, I had an experience which taught me an important lesson about Secret Number Five and the power of my mind to create my reality. I was the featured speaker at a convention and gave a presentation before a large crowd. As usual, my mind found someone who didn't seem to be pleased with me—a women sitting near the front in the side section. She sat through my whole talk without smiling and sighing heavily, as if she couldn't wait to leave. She even glanced down at her watch several times, which only made me feel worse.

After the speech, I was autographing my books for people at a table in the lobby, when I noticed the woman approaching me. My first thought was, *"Oh, no, she's one of those critics who's going to tell me what is wrong with my ideas."* So I braced myself for the conversation.

"I know you're busy," she began, "but I couldn't

leave without thanking you. I'm on my way back to the hospital to see my husband. He had a stroke a few days ago and isn't doing very well. I've been by his side ever since, but I couldn't miss your presentation because I'm one of your biggest fans. I just want you to know that everything you said touched me so deeply. I felt like you were speaking directly to me and that God sent you here today to give me hope and inspiration." Then, as tears poured down her face, the woman reached out to offer me a hug.

As I held her trembling body, I vowed that I would never forget that moment, which contained so many important lessons for me. For all these years, my mind had projected my own insecurities and self-criticisms onto members of my audiences who, like this woman, probably were sitting there in emotional or physical pain, or with worries too great to allow them to even smile. My selective attention was trying to create a problem where there simply wasn't one. And I also saw that even if someone didn't enjoy my seminar, there would always be many other people who were touched by my work and I could only do my best and let that be good enough.

After that incident, my whole experience of public speaking changed. I decided to use my selective attention to find the people in the audience who were smiling the most, obviously enjoying what I had to say and sending me lots of positive energy. The more I focused on them, the more relaxed and dynamic I became. As I gained more confidence, I'd experiment with finding those other, less enthusiastic faces again. This time, however, instead of allowing my mind to imagine that the person didn't like me, I'd remind myself that perhaps this person needed *my* love more than I needed his or hers. And I'd send extra smiles and energy in that person's direction.

The nature of your mind is to have selective attention. There's nothing wrong with that tendency. So why not use it to your advantage? Look for what you want your mind to be focused on and steer it in that direction.

Learn to refocus your mind
in the direction *you* want it to go.

What You Didn't Know About Negative Thoughts

We are trampled most often by forces we ourselves create.
WILLIAM SHAKESPEARE

Most of us would agree that it's not healthy for us to harbor negative thoughts about ourselves, even if we have a difficult time sticking to this resolution. However, when it comes to negative thoughts about others, it's often harder for us to see the harm, or to relinquish the habit of being critical, judgmental. Why? Because feeling angry and judgmental gives us a temporary rush of power, a false sense of strength and aggression, as if by thinking harshly about someone we are actually hurting him or her. This couldn't be further from the truth.

**Your negative thoughts about others don't hurt them—
they hurt you.**

I think we have the false notion that a negative thought
about someone is like an arrow that we send toward a
target, hoping it will cause hurt. If we are angry with
someone who we think has done despicable things and
we sit around thinking awful thoughts about him, we
may feel a secret sense of satisfaction, as if those thoughts
sent in his direction will somehow wound him or make
him feel bad, as if each negative thought is a triumph on
our part. "I hate you," we think to ourselves, "and
therefore, I win!"

But the truth is very different from this conclusion.
Your negative thoughts are not like arrows that will deliver harm to another. Instead, they are like balloons tied
to strings, and they float over your head, keeping that
negativity in your own energy field. Each time you indulge in negativity about someone, you are polluting
your own consciousness. It's as if those negative thoughts
are emotional smog, hanging in a cloud over you.

Did you know that you can see people's thoughts?
It's true—just look at their faces and feel their energy
and you will be able to tell a lot about the quality of their
thoughts. I'm not particularly talking about seeing with
your physical eyes, but with your inner eyes. People who
indulge in a lot of negative thinking tend to look almost
as if there's a gray cloud above their heads. When you
are around them, you feel as if a thunderstorm could

erupt at any moment. On the other hand, people who fill their minds with a lot of positive, loving thoughts look radiant, shining, as if there is a natural glow emanating from deep within them. If you think of any great beings you know and admire, you'll notice that they are naturally luminous.

This understanding sheds a totally new light on the power of your mind to make you beautiful or unattractive. This is what is meant by inner beauty, that energetic vibration created when you are filled with positive and loving thoughts about yourself and others. If it's true that you end up looking like you think, then you may have found a new motivation for creating a more positive mind!

Here's another important secret about the mind: Not only do your thoughts fill you with an inner vibration, but they radiate a vibration that attracts similar energies to it.

> Your thoughts are like magnets:
> they will attract similar energies.

We all know this intuitively. When you walk around with a lot of unresolved anger, you tend to attract angry situations and hostile people. When you walk around feeling nervous and worried, things tend to go wrong and you make everyone around you feel nervous, as well. When you walk around feeling positive and loving, you bring out the love in others and create harmony around you. This is another reason to work on making friends with your mind.

Becoming the Witness

Do you know that there's a part of you that watches everything that goes on in your life like a cosmic spectator? It's called *the witness*. It is that still, silent part of your being that is just pure consciousness. It's not your mind, or your emotions, or your senses, or your experiences, but it's that which is *aware* of all of these. It's what makes you know that you are awake, that you are *you* and not someone else. It is your true, great self.

Most of us become so identified with our thoughts or feelings that we forget we even are the witness; we forget that we even have a source of consciousness inside of us. As I mentioned earlier, it would be like forgetting that you're the one watching the movie in the theater and thinking instead that you're the actor on the screen. *Remembering to include yourself in what you're watching about your life is the key to gaining control over your mind.*

Each time you perceive anything or experience anything in life, there are two components to the experience: a) *what* you are noticing, and b) *who* is noticing. Perhaps you notice that you're upset. *What* you are noticing is that you're feeling unhappy. But *who* is noticing your unhappiness? It's your witness, your consciousness. Perhaps you notice that you are frightened. But *who* is noticing your fear? It is your witness.

Many ancient spiritual traditions talk about the witness as the true self, that pure awareness that is our connection to spirit, to God. There is always a *you* quietly watching the drama of your life. The key is to identify with *who* is watching, rather than *what* you are watching. This allows you to go through life strengthened by that inner anchor, that inner stability. When you practice watching your life from the witness, you'll be able to watch your mind and all of its activities without being affected by every thought you have. No matter what is happening to you on the outside, you are calm on the inside.

Learn to watch your thoughts without identifying with your thoughts.

Here's how to practice witness consciousness. Let's say I become aware that after a conversation with my boyfriend, I'm feeling hurt. Something he said upset me. If I practice witness consciousness, I can pull back from the drama and ask myself to notice what is going on: "I am feeling hurt. My mind is full of fearful thoughts. I am becoming more tense as I let these thoughts continue. Lots of sad emotions are coming up."

Identifying with the witness allows me to put some distance between myself and my mind. Instead of saying, "I feel terrible," I can say, "I am watching my mind having terrible thoughts. What can I do about it?" Suddenly, *I* am not the problem. Nothing is *wrong* with me.

I am just dealing with a situation. Now I can control my reaction to what is happening and respond wisely, instead of letting myself get lost in an emotional storm.

When you watch your mind, you can begin to take control over it and make it work for you and not against you. You can start by simply noticing when you are upset or anxious or less than happy and asking yourself this simple question:

"What is my mind doing right now?"

Just asking this question pulls you back from being absorbed in your mind and distinguishes you as separate from your mind. You aren't your thoughts. You are the one watching your thoughts, the one noticing that you don't like your thoughts, the witness. And the answer to "What is my mind doing?" will probably be that your mind is thinking negative thoughts that are making you feel bad. Now that you know what your mind is doing, you can either invite it to do something else, or just compassionately watch it processing its hurt.

To help me make friends with my mind and practice the principles of Secret Number Five, I have little signs in different places all over my house that say: WHAT IS YOUR MIND DOING? There's one on each of my phones, one on my computer, one on my refrigerator. Whenever I find myself feeling unhappy, that's the first thing I ask myself: "Barbara, what is your mind doing right now?" The answer is always revealing and is the first step toward my changing the direction of my mind and taking charge of my reality in the moment.

Watching the Thought Parade

Sometimes, when you're going through an unusually difficult period, it can be overwhelming to watch your mind because there is so much taking place. Last summer I found that I just couldn't get my mind to slow down. It seemed as if there was this constant barrage of emotions and thoughts that was exhausting to keep up with. One day I was sitting quietly, trying to sort through all of my mental craziness and noticing a group of thoughts that was very familiar, but very unwelcome—panicky thoughts. "What if this happened, what if that happened?" *"Oh, it's those guys again,"* I groaned to myself. Suddenly, an image popped into my mind, that of a large boat filled with all of these panicky people running back and forth on the deck worrying themselves sick, complaining to each other. I actually found myself amused to think of a boatload of these people stuck together on this vessel that was cruising past me on the ocean. Instantly, I calmed down as I imagined myself as that deep, silent ocean, noticing a boat that happened to be passing by on my surface.

I decided to sit for a while and see if I could apply this technique to other thoughts. And sure enough, more boats came. There was the boat filled with a whole bunch of serious, responsible people dressed in business suits who were waving at each other lists of all the things they needed to get done—they weren't having much fun. There was the boat of sad little girls, all crying and feeling sorry for themselves and begging someone to come rescue them. There was the boat of rowdy, angry people, shouting about all the unfair things that had happened to them—they were a wild bunch. On and on they came, a whole flotilla of boats, each containing groups of thoughts from my very active mind.

After a few minutes of witnessing my thoughts like this, I found myself smiling. What I had noticed was that if I didn't get involved with each boatload of thoughts, they would, indeed, pass by and disappear. I use this technique regularly, particularly when I need to lighten up or when there are so many thoughts in my head that I can't sort through them. "O.K., everyone on your boats!" I yell, and then I sit back and watch the parade.

How to Stop Judging and Battling with Your Thoughts

When people ask me, "How can I get rid of all my negative thoughts," my answer is, "You can't." Thoughts of all kinds will always be there. That's the nature of the mind and the nature of the senses, to notice, to respond. So in learning to watch your thoughts, you need to make sure you aren't judging your thoughts.

**Judging your thoughts is a totally unproductive use of your energy.
It just adds another negative thought on top of the pile.**

Making friends with your mind doesn't mean making your mind wrong for its thoughts. It means lovingly steering your mind in a more positive direction. Many times we end up in a battle with our minds because we are unhappy with what they're doing. Then we end up criticizing our minds for being critical! Pretty ironic, isn't it? Judging yourself for having unpleasant or disturbing thoughts just perpetuates the vicious cycle of negativity and you end up sinking into a downward spiral of depression and despair.

It's not your thoughts that are the problem. It's your reactions to your thoughts that are the problem. What if you were to watch your thoughts in the same way you watch television? As you switch channels, all kinds of stuff passes before your eyes, information, drama, humor, romance. You notice what's on the screen and decide if you want to stay with that channel or not. You don't get upset if you find yourself on a channel you don't like. You simply switch.

Learning to witness your thoughts is like this. You begin to watch your mind with all of its fascinating dramas and reactions, knowing that there are hundreds of channels available to you. **And you remember that you are not what you see on those channels—you are the watcher, the person holding the remote control in your hand.**

So what happens if you find yourself tuned into a channel you don't like, say, the Horror Channel, where every imaginable fear you have about your life plays continually over and over again? You can say to yourself:

"Oh, look, I'm having all kinds of fearful thoughts."

You will notice that, just like on TV, what's playing on that channel in your mind will be effective in making you actually *feel* anxious and fearful. That's O.K. Just watch the process and remind yourself:

> I am not my thoughts.
> I am not my reactions to my thoughts.
> I am the one who is watching my thoughts.

Identify yourself as the one noticing the thoughts. Soon, those particular thoughts will pass. The channel has changed on its own, or perhaps you've been successful in switching it. And then your mind will go on to the next thing, but you didn't get caught up in its drama.

For many years, I've given personal growth seminars to large groups of people. One of the processes we include in the seminar is *sharing*, times when people can stand up and talk about what they are experiencing, what emotions are coming up for them, what insights they've received. Part of the seminar leader's job is to make everyone feel good about honoring their feelings, no matter what they are, and so it's customary in my seminar and in many other people's to say, "Thank you for sharing" after the person finishes.

Sometimes when I am witnessing my own particularly dramatic, panicky, or angry thoughts, as if I'm watching a hysterical child having a tantrum, I will say to my mind, "Thank you for sharing, Barbara." It's like saying, "I hear you. I understand. Your feelings and reactions are not wrong or right. They just are."

Whose Mind Is It Anyway?

D o you know that there are other people living inside your head? If you don't believe me, watch your thoughts for a while and you'll discover that many of them aren't even yours to begin with. They belong to your parents, your family, your spouse, your friends, society, religious leaders. These thoughts often express themselves as the *shoulds* and *ought tos* of your mind.

I call these *alien thoughts*. It's as if they have invaded your consciousness and taken over your brain. Then, they give you secret commands from inside. The trouble with these alien thoughts is you never know when they will pop up.

For instance, you're getting dressed for work. You put on an outfit you like a lot. Suddenly, you hear a voice in your head say, "You're not going to wear *that* are you?" Who is it? *It's your mother!* Her thought is somehow in your mind. Or you're out on a date with a man you really like and are about to open up and share some intimate feelings, and you hear a voice say, "You are too intense and emotional—this will turn him off." Who is it? *It's your ex-husband.*

This is a great time to use that "Thank you for sharing" technique. The alternative is to start a mental battle between your thoughts and the alien thoughts, and that's just going to be exhausting and frustrating. *And the more you resist these thoughts, the stronger they usually get.*

The next time you notice yourself having unpleasant thoughts, ask yourself:

"Whose thought is this, mine or someone else's?"

You may be shocked at the answer. Maybe the voices in your head belong to one of your parents, or to your ex-boyfriend, or your sister. No wonder you're feeling so uncomfortable. You have other people's voices telling you what to do and what they think of you, other people's ideas filling your mind.

When you notice alien invaders in your mind, don't panic. We all have them, and you may never get rid of them. Empowering yourself means not letting them run the show, however, and making your own voice the strongest and clearest.

Breaking the Habit of Negative Thinking

We saw earlier how our negative self-talk turns our mind into an enemy rather than a friend. But how do we break this insidious habit? If you're serious about starting to love yourself more and criticize yourself less, I invite you to use the following technique, which will dramatically reduce the number of negative thoughts you have about yourself.

I came up with this idea years ago when I was working with one of my seminar students. She had continually complained to me that she could not stop thinking negative thoughts about herself, no matter how hard she tried. "I'm desperate, Barbara," she pleaded. "I almost feel like my mind is addicted to putting me down, and I just can't control it."

Now, I knew that her mind, like yours and mine, wasn't inherently negative—it just had gotten fixated onto a negative habit. So how to break it? The trick was to somehow make the process of thinking negative thoughts very unappealing to the mind itself. Suddenly, I had an idea.

I asked this woman if she was willing to do anything to break this habit. "Yes, anything!" she insisted. So I told her that for the next week, she was going to record every time she had a negative thought about herself by making a line in a notebook. And that at the end of each day, she would count up the lines and for each line, she would put a certain amount of money into a jar or a box. For instance, if she decided on twenty-five cents and at the end of that day she'd had forty-eight negative thoughts about herself, she would put twenty-five cents times forty-eight into the jar, or twelve dollars. If she decided on one dollar per negative thought, she'd put forty-eight dollars in the jar.

"This sounds interesting," she said. "But what happens to the money?"

"That's where the motivation comes in," I explained with a smile. *"At the end of the week, you add up all the money you've put aside from every negative thought about yourself, and you are going to give that money to the person you most dislike in the whole world!"*

"What?" she shrieked

"That's right," I answered. "Think of someone you just can't stand, or someone who has really hurt you, or perhaps someone you don't know who represents a cause you find totally offensive. It has to be the last person in the world to whom you'd want to give money. You need to make a promise to yourself that you will give that person all the money from your negative thought fund. Does anyone come to mind?"

She grimaced. "Oh yeah," she replied. "My ex-boyfriend who cheated on me."

"Do you like the idea of giving him money?"

She gave me a searing look. "What do you think?"

"Good, so you'll be motivated. Now, how much do you want to put up?"

"O.K., I really want to break this habit, so I'll go for a dollar a thought."

We agreed that she would start the next day.

By lunch time on the following day, this woman called me in a panic. "Barbara, I already have twenty-five lines!" she explained. "At this rate, I'll be giving this jerk hundreds of dollars!"

"What will he do with the money?" I asked.

"Oh, he'll probably buy sexy lingerie for his bitchy little girlfriend and take her on some trip."

"Well, then, you'd better pay more attention to your thoughts!"

That night, she called me again, this time in tears. "How much do you owe today?" I asked.

"Seventy-four dollars," she said in a trembling voice.

"Do you want tomorrow to turn out the same way?"

"*No!*" she said with determination. "If I don't change things, I'll end up giving him hundreds of dollars."

"O.K., so if you don't want to pay the price for your

negative thoughts, wake up tomorrow and take control of your mind. Watch it carefully, don't get lazy or distracted, and before it can form the negative thought completely, change it into a positive one."

I didn't hear from her all day, but the next night she called, and I knew by the tone in her voice that something had changed. "I'm doing it!" she announced triumphantly. "I was so pissed at the idea of giving my ex money that I watched my mind like a hawk. And I noticed something amazing—my negative thoughts don't just pop up. I could actually feel them starting to form. This morning, I'd made a wrong turn on the way to work, and all of a sudden I could feel my mind wanting to say, 'You are so stupid. Now you're going to be late,' but it was still just an impulse, and I thought of my ex and consciously said to myself, 'It's O.K., you're only a minute out of your way.' It felt great! Then in my staff meeting, I made a suggestion that no one really liked that much. And I could see my mind running over to grab the situation and use it to beat myself off, but I got there first and said, 'Good for you. You spoke up and participated. That's what counts.'

"Catching myself began to become a game in itself," she continued, "and I was so motivated by not wanting to send him money that I really concentrated on watching my mind. I never realized that there is always a moment there when I do have the choice about what direction my mind will go in. By the end of the day, I only had eight marks, and I felt so powerful and really proud of myself!"

This woman kept her commitment to go through

the entire week in this way. By Friday night, she had ninety-six marks, pretty good for someone who used to have ninety-six negative thoughts about herself in just one day! But she'd learned that she did, indeed, have control over her mind, and that having positive thoughts about herself instead of negative ones simply required a shift in her awareness, some practice, and the commitment to start loving herself. And yes, she did send her ex-boyfriend a check for ninety-six dollars, and she told me that when she put it in the envelope, she caught herself about to think something negative and instead thought, "I'm grateful to this person for motivating me to change my life!" And no, she didn't explain what the money was for!

I didn't share this story simply because it is entertaining. This technique really works. Your habit of negative thinking will not break itself. You need to intervene and change the pattern. You can do it!

And if you get an unexplained check in the mail from someone in your past, well, you'll know they probably read this book too!

You don't have to keep track of your thoughts and put aside money if you feel ready to make friends with your mind. Just begin the very simple practice of noticing your negative thoughts and replacing each one with a positive thought right in the moment. This is called *introducing a positive alternative*, and it's the best way to retrain your mind. Have you ever tried to paper-train a puppy? When the puppy pees on the rug, you don't yell at it—you pick it up and show it an alternative spot where it is supposed to pee, and in this way, the puppy learns what you want it to.

It's the same with your mind. When you notice your mind having a little "mental accident" on the rug of your consciousness, thinking thoughts you wish would stop, ask yourself:

> **"What is another thought I could have that would make me happier and be more supportive?"**

Then, replace the old thought with a positive alternative. If you find yourself thinking, "My boss will probably hate what I have to say in the meeting," change the thought to, "People enjoy listening to me because I express myself with clarity and wisdom." Change "You look terrible today," to "I am a beautiful person inside and out." Change "I can't believe how overwhelmed you are," to "I am very courageous to be taking on so much right now."

You don't even have to believe what you are saying at first. Just changing your thoughts will instantly begin to shift how you feel. And don't forget to do this out loud as well as in your conversations with people. My friends and I try to remind each other of this principle and whenever we notice the other saying something negative, we suggest a positive alternative. This is a great way to support the people you love in creating a new, positive thinking habit.

It's also helpful to have a special thought you use as a reminder of life's highest truths—kind of an all-purpose thought you can focus on any time you need some inspiration, strength, or guidance. This is the principle behind religious rituals of repeating phrases, reciting the rosary, or using a mantra as in eastern traditions: giving the mind, whose nature it is to think, the highest thing to think about. You can use a technique from a spiritual tradition or create your own phrase. I came up with a phrase that really works for me by cutting through all of my negativity and reminding me of the ultimate truth as I understand it:

"God loves me and wants me to be happy."

When I am going through a hard time and even witnessing my thoughts isn't giving me relief, I will repeat this phrase to myself, either out loud or silently, infusing my mind with its truth. After a while, I notice myself relaxing, easing up on my insistence to make everything feel better right away, and breathing more easily. It almost feels as if my mind is starving for a higher thought in these challenging moments and gobbles it up as soon as I introduce it.

Learning to Let Go of What Your Mind Doesn't Need

Thirty years ago, my first spiritual teacher told me this classic story:

Once there were two monks who lived in a monastery high up in the Himalayas in India. These monks had taken vows of poverty, celibacy, and service, and spent most of their time with the others in the order totally removed from the world and studying the ancient scriptures. It came to pass that these two monks had to take a journey down to the city to gather some supplies. And so they set off from their mountain home.

After several days of traveling, they came to a wide river filled with rapidly rushing water. The river lay between them and their destination and so they prepared to wade across it. Suddenly, they noticed a beautiful young woman pacing back and forth along the riverbanks. When she noticed the monks, she quickly approached them, bowing in the usual respectful manner.

"Oh, revered ones," she began. "Surely God sent you to me. I must get across this river to find milk for my children, but it is too high and I am too short and a poor swimmer at that. Surely I will drown if I attempt a crossing. I have been praying for a miracle and now you have arrived. Would you be so kind as to carry me on your back to the other side?"

The older of the two monks smiled at this lovely creature and said, "We are servants of God. Of course we will help you." And with that, he bent over, offered her his back, hoisted her up as high as he could, and began to ford the river, the younger monk following close behind with a scowl on his face.

Halfway across the rushing river, the older monk's energy began to fail him. "Brother," he called out to the younger monk, "it is your turn to take her the rest of the way." The woman was transferred to the back of the second monk and they continued across until they were safely on the opposite shore. The woman thanked the monks profusely, touched their feet in respect, and went on her way.

The two monks walked down the path toward the city and the younger monk began to speak. "Brother, I am horrified," he said. "We have taken vows never to touch a woman, and yet you offered to carry that one on your back and insisted that I do the same! What would people say? What if someone saw us? Oh, this is just a tragedy." The older monk did not respond.

An hour passed and the younger monk piped up again. "How could you do this?" he cried. "We are tainted, ruined. All of our austerities are for naught. We have touched the flesh of a woman, and a beautiful one at that! What will we tell the head of the monastery?" Again, the older monk was silent.

Another hour passed and the younger monk now began to shout, "Brother, aren't you listening?" he cried, tearing at his hair. "We have sinned against God! We are doomed! We will be reborn in our next life as toads or vermin!"

The older monk, who had been listening to this tirade for miles, turned slowly towards the younger initiate and said, "Brother, I left that woman back at the river-bank hours ago. Why are you still carrying her?"

At times, you may find yourself feeling like that young monk, carrying something in your mind that you just can't let go of. It could be worry about a situation you can't do anything about. It could be a reaction to something painful that happened to you. It could be a problem to which you just can't seem to find a solution. Your mind, whose nature it is to analyze, can fixate on these issues, so that it feels like you can't think about anything else.

I experience this kind of mental broken record frequently. I have a very analytical mind, and one which likes to know the answers to things. So when I can't figure something out, it makes me very uncomfortable. I've learned the hard way that there are times when we have to do what a dear friend of mine suggests:

Just drop it.

I'm not talking about suppressing your feelings or ignoring problems, but about breaking the cycle of obsessively thinking about things you can't control in that moment. To just let go. We talked about this in Secret Number Three, to stop resisting and go with the flow, and it applies to the mind, as well.

How do you do this? If you are aware that there's a big battle raging in your mind between different thoughts and attitudes, just notice that it's happening and tell your mind you'll check back in with it later. For now, you're taking a break. Walk away from the fight—don't step right into the middle of it. It may be that you are unconsciously sorting something out and you don't even need to know the details. Often you will find that by just letting go of your resistance to what your mind is doing, your mind will calm down.

Whenever I am feeling overwhelmed by negative thoughts, I create a ceremony for letting go of them in my mind. I imagine myself walking into a beautiful and mystical temple, the temple of my own heart. Before me sits my spiritual teacher, or for you, any symbol of spirit that you resonate with—a person, a light, an object. And in the center of the temple is a sacred fire. I stand before the fire and imagine that in my hands are bundles of all those negative thoughts or emotions I want to release, and I offer them to the sacrificial fire, asking that I be free of their influence and I am left feeling only love. I imagine dropping the thought bundles into the fire and seeing the flames rise up to swallow them. Then I pay my respects to my teacher and ask for strength and blessings and my visualization is over.

I have had very profound experiences of healing performing this inner ceremony. Remember, Secret Number Five says that your mind creates your reality, so why not use it to heal and purify the mind itself?

•   •   •

Once my spiritual teacher asked a large group of people: "Do you want to know your future?" Everyone sat on the edge of their chairs, anticipating some cosmic announcement about our souls' destiny or some mystical prediction. She smiled, and said, "Look at your mind."

How simple, and yet this has been the teaching throughout the ages. *As we think, so we become.* You've been given this great and mysterious gift of the mind. Like all tools of power, you can use it to hurt yourself or to cut through the confusion in your life and remember the higher truths. You can use it to destroy your happiness or to build new experiences of joy. You have the freedom to choose what you will think, to change the thoughts you are having now into those that are more supportive, more beneficial, to create the reality you want, moment by moment.

Yes, you are the sorceress
who can perform these feats of magic in your life.
It's all up to you.

Fear Will Steal Your Aliveness— Make Your Courage Bigger than Your Fear

We have met the enemy and they are us.

POGO

I magine that you had a person in your life who followed you around twenty-four hours a day, filling you with anxiety, destroying your confidence, and discouraging you from doing the things you really wanted to do. Every time you were about to make a change or take a risk, this person would say, "I wouldn't do that if I were you. What if you fail? What if you get hurt? All kinds of bad things might happen if you go in that direction." Imagine that before each conversation you had with friends, family, or loved ones, this person would pull you aside and caution you: "If you open up, you might get rejected. Watch what you say! Don't trust anyone!" Imagine that each time you considered taking action on any of your desires, personal or professional, this person would whisper: "You'll be sorry if you do this. It's going to turn out horribly."

As you read this you may be thinking, "Well, I'd never tolerate someone like this in my life. I'd never put up with someone talking to me this way." But the truth is, you probably already do—it's your *fear*.

Fear is like an emotional roommate that lives with you day and night. It talks to you, manipulates you, and tries to convince you to avoid doing or expressing anything that may cause you any kind of discomfort or involve any sort of risk. It says, "You can't . . ." and "You shouldn't. . . ." It eats away at your confidence and your self-esteem. It tells you not to act, not to reach out, not to try, not to trust, not to move. It steals life right out from under you.

Whether you've thought about it this way or not, you have a relationship with your fear and it's one of the most important relationships in your life. Take a moment and ask yourself:

> What is my relationship with my fear?
> Do I let it dominate me?
> Do I let it talk me out of my dreams?
> Do I let it stop me from being the powerful woman I want to be?
> Do I talk back to my fear up to a point and then just fall apart and give in to its demands?
> Do I know how to stay focused on my goals in spite of the efforts my fear makes to pull me off track?
> Who is in control in this relationship most of the time, me or fear?

Fear is one of your most powerful inner enemies. It is a force that can sabotage your happiness. How does fear do this? It keeps you stuck in what's not working. It prevents you from growing. It creates separation between you and other people. It talks you out of your dreams. It keeps you stagnant, frozen, unable to become all you were meant to be.

Right now in your life, there are things you want to

do that you're not doing, changes you want to make that you're not making, conversations you need to have that you're not having, risks you want to take that you're not taking. Maybe you've been longing to do some of these things for weeks, months, even years, but you end up procrastinating. What's stopping you? *Your fear.*

In chapter three, we began talking about how as we grow and encounter change, it is inevitable that we experience fear. It is fear that keeps us standing on that cliff when we know we need to leap to the other side. But fear does more than just hold you back—it steals your aliveness, your passion, your freedom, by shutting down your heart.

How Fear Robs You of Your Freedom

Think about what your life would be like if you were a slave. From moment to moment, you are told what you can and cannot do. You are not allowed to have any desires, dreams, or wishes for success and happiness—your "master" forbids it. If you try and suggest that you would like to do something that will bring you fulfillment, you are beaten down with harsh words, told you aren't good enough, that you don't deserve it, and that you should be grateful just to stay in the place you are. After a while, you stop even having any dreams or longings and accept your fate that you will never be free, so you might as well make the best of it.

This is a horrifying possibility, isn't it? Well, imagine

that the master I described is called "Fear," that force inside of you that keeps you from taking risks, making changes, and living as the great soul you truly are. Can you see how fear controls you? How it talks you out of your dreams? How it intimidates you into not moving from exactly where you are?

None of us would tolerate being enslaved to another person and yet we tolerate the presence of fear in our lives. Fear stops you from being who you want to be, doing what you want to do, loving as you want to love. *It robs you of your freedom.*

The extent to which you allow fear to control your life is the extent to which you are living as a prisoner.

Many of us know we have fear in certain areas of our life, but we'd probably be astonished to uncover all the other, sometimes subtle ways we allow fear to hold us back. Here are just some of the statements you might be able to make about how you allow fear to control you:

I put off doing my most difficult projects at work until the last minute because I'm afraid I won't do a good job.

I don't ask my husband for what I like in bed and just let the resentment build up.

I avoid people I know are upset with me, hoping not to have to be confronted.

I resist calling my father, since I know he is very ill and I'm afraid to hear bad news.

I say *yes* to what other people want me to do, rather than setting boundaries, because I don't want them to be upset with me.

I edit everything I say around important people since I don't want to sound dumb or inexperienced.

I tell myself that certain things I want to do aren't really that important, rather than admitting how frustrated I am with myself and going out and taking action.

I don't stand up for myself with my boyfriend when we are out with other people and he criticizes me, for fear of ruining our evening by getting him angry.

I butter up my supervisor at work even when I know he is wrong, rather than offering some constructive suggestions.

I have a hard time committing to planning fun things in the future like vacations, since I'm so afraid when the time comes, I won't be able to afford it.

Think about how much mental and emotional energy it takes for you to do even one of the above and how uncomfortable it makes you feel. You need to begin to understand that the more fear controls your decisions and behavior, the more it drains you of your energy, your enthusiasm, your passion. And there is no greater bondage than living life in constant fear—fear of failure, fear of change, fear of rejection, fear of making mistakes, fear of taking a risk.

Understanding Your Secret Inner Battle

All growth includes struggle and victory—the triumph of the new over the old, the conquest of the past by the present. And when the growth we're talking about is personal and spiritual, the battles occur inside of you. Perhaps you didn't know it, but every day you fight hundreds of these inner battles. It's the battle between the woman you are used to being and the new woman who is trying to emerge, the battle between confusion and clarity, the battle between the forces of fear and the forces of freedom.

Your inner battle is a power struggle between two parts of your being, one that represents *destructive use of power*, and the other that represents *constructive use of power*. It's the battle between your fear and the courageous part of you that I call your visionary.

Who is your visionary?

It is your most clear, loving, and wise self.

It is your enlightened mind that is naturally in tune with these secrets about life.

It is that which fills your heart with hope and inspires you to keep going.

It is the voice that encourages you to take a chance and leap, and it is the force that picks you up after you have fallen and gives you the courage to leap again.

It is the dreamer and the creator and the holder of all your happy endings.

It is the true source of your power, positivity, and contentment.

It is the part of you that shines your light to the world.

It is who you really are.

Each of us has fear and a visionary living inside of us. Like two ancient warriors fighting over the same territory, your fear and your visionary use your day-to-day life as a battleground, each trying to take control over the other, each trying to be the force inside you that wields the true power.

To understand how to win the battle with your fear, you need to understand the true source of your fear. So let's take a journey back in time, back to when you were just a newborn infant.

When you first came into this world, you were perfect: You had no self-esteem problems—in fact, you believed that you were the most important person on earth. You had no fear, no anger, no mistrust. You were full of confidence and optimism. Most of all, your heart was filled only with love, love for yourself and anyone you met. Babies are such loving, trusting creatures because they haven't yet been exposed to that experience called "life" and the hurts, disappointments, and rejections it inevitably brings.

Back in those days, you had no fear in your personality. You *were* the visionary, full of hope and dreams and a powerfully motivating force inside your heart that gave you the courage to take enormous risks every day— learning to walk, to talk, to explore, to try new things (for, after all, everything was a new thing!). There was no inner battle, no struggle within you for power, because there was only the visionary.

The reason your visionary was so alive when you were small is:

The visionary within you feeds on love.

An environment of love always helps your visionary to grow strong and courageous, just like sunlight helps a plant to thrive. Most of us received some degree of love, nurturing, and positive attention as infants and small children, thus making it a time when our visionary dominated our awareness of who we were.

And then one day, probably when you were still quite young, something very disturbing happened to you—you were hurt or rejected. Maybe it was the first time you heard the word *no* from one of your parents; maybe it was the first time you fell down and injured yourself; maybe it was the first time someone yelled at you or didn't think you were perfect just the way you are. No matter when this event occurred in your life, whether at the age of six days old or six months, it had the same effect: *you experienced pain.* And like most human beings, you hated pain and wanted to do everything you could to avoid experiencing it again.

It was at that moment that your fear was born. A part of your mind saw you in pain and reasoned: "I, as a human brain, have been programmed to do everything I can to protect this human being from harm and make sure this person survives for as long as possible. I notice that this experience (reaching out to Daddy for attention; asking to play with the other children; expressing something disturbing that you're feeling, etc.) has caused this human being pain and discomfort. That is not good for her survival. Therefore, from now on, I will do everything I can to make sure she does not engage in this same behavior or get in this same situation again."

And this is exactly what happened. The next time you thought about asking someone if you could be her friend, you felt more cautious, afraid she'd say no. The next time you considered being honest with one of your parents, you held back, afraid they'd get angry with you again. *Your fear had been successful in preventing you from doing what it thought could potentially hurt you.*

Why did your mind decide to dissuade you from doing certain things? *Because the true nature of the mind is love, and it loves you.* What technique does the mind use to "protect" you from experiences it thinks will harm you? It uses fear.

> **Fear is created out of love by your own mind to protect you from pain.**

This is an amazing revelation: The source of all of your fear, therefore, is not self-hatred or low self-esteem—it's love. Fear is just a device your mind uses to try and warn you away from situations it feels might hurt you, based on ones that have hurt you in the past. Remember: your fear first came into existence *not* to be your enemy, but your protector from pain. However, it ended up protecting you from happiness as well, sabotaging your dreams and stifling your freedom.

> **Fear pretends to protect us from harm when it is actually robbing us of our passion for life.**

It's as if your fear is like a worried mother who sees her child reaching for what appears to be a sharp knife and screams, "Stop! Don't go any farther!" Only it's not a knife—it's a banana! This is the problem with our fear: many times, what our fear *thinks* is dangerous isn't actually threatening at all. There's something familiar about the situation and it reminds the mind of a past time when you *were* in emotional danger, so it jumps to the conclusion that this, too, is one of those times and enlists fear to keep you from going any farther.

Is It Really a Snake, or Is Your Fear
Playing Tricks on You?

Many years ago at one of my first meditation retreats, I heard this classic story from the Indian scriptures that has been used throughout the ages to teach seekers about the nature of the mind and the way it superimposes reality onto that which is only an illusion.

It was late at night in a small village in India. One of the villagers had been visiting a sick neighbor several miles away and was walking down the very dark and unlit road to return home. Now, this area was known to be frequented by dangerous and deadly snakes and the man was already very frightened as he made his way along the path. "What if I encounter a snake?" he worried, trembling at just the thought of one of these terrible creatures.

Suddenly, in the dim light, the man noticed something large and thick coiled up in the middle of the road. "It's a snake!" he cried aloud, as he began to scream and run in circles. "Help! Help! Someone come quickly! A snake is about to kill me!"

Another villager happened to be not too far down the road from the first man and when he heard the commotion, he came quickly toward the sound of the shouting.

"What's the matter, friend?" he asked.

"Look! Look!" shrieked the first man, pointing a shaking finger at the coiled-up serpent. "It's a snake!"

The second villager was carrying a lamp and he cautiously approached the shadow in the road, held up the light, and looked. And there before him, he saw a coil of thick rope that someone had mistakenly dropped on the path.

"Friend, calm yourself," the villager said. "There is no snake here—only a rope. Fear has made your mind play a trick on you."

How many times have you mistaken a rope, or even a string, for a snake in your own life, becoming fearful about something that turns out to be nothing at all? You run around, stirring everything and everyone up with your fear, trampling on your state of peace and contentment, when all you had to do was to look more carefully at what appeared to be a snake and discover that it was only an illusion. This is how fear drains your vital energy, your aliveness, using it to immobilize you rather than to uplift and inspire you.

There is a metaphysical principle that says fear is:

False Evidence Appearing Real.

The snake appeared to be real, but it wasn't. It was false evidence of something to be afraid of. This is the way it is with so much of what we fear. If we found the courage to look more closely, to hold up the light of our own wisdom to what appeared to be blocking our way, we would see that what frightens us often doesn't even exist.

Life will always be full of ropes that appear to be snakes. Perhaps they are even put in our path to test our courage and strengthen our clarity. And the natural re-action to being confronted with what appears to threaten us is always going to be fear. So the solution is not to try and get rid of your fear but to deal with it differently.

> Fear does not go away.
> Your attitude toward it changes.

Every time you are confronted with fear, you have a choice as to who is going to be in charge—your visionary, that courageous part of you, or your fear.

Here is the sixth principle:

SECRET NUMBER SIX:

**FEAR WILL STEAL YOUR
ALIVENESS—
MAKE YOUR COURAGE BIGGER
THAN YOUR FEAR**

The great philosopher and writer Mark Twain said, "Courage is resistance to fear, mastery of fear—not absence of fear." The secret for changing your relationship with fear isn't to try and destroy it—it's to make your courage, your true knowing, much bigger than your fear. It's to make your dreams and your vision much bigger than your fear. It's to make your love for yourself much bigger than your fear.

You can do it!
You are more powerful than you think you are.

Are You Misinterpreting Your Fear?

Fear is a natural reaction to moving closer to the truth.
PEMA CHÖDRÖN

We all have many misconceptions about fear, misconceptions that keep us stuck in fear much longer than we need to be. *The first of these is that the presence of fear means that we are doing something wrong.* For instance, suppose you've met a man you really like and are becoming more and more intimate with him. You wake up one morning and realize you have a lot of fear about getting involved in a relationship. How should you interpret that fear? Is it a sign that you aren't supposed to be with this guy? Does the presence of fear mean you are making a mistake?

The answer is probably: *No!* Your fear is a sign that you have gone beyond your comfort zone, beyond your usual answers. It signals that you are entering uncharted territory, that you are facing the unknown, that you are opening yourself up to a new emotional adventure. Actually, it is a sign that something exciting, something astonishing is happening to you.

Your fear just means you're having a human reaction to contemplating change and growth—that's all. It's natural for all of us to experience fear when we encounter something new. We just need to listen to what the fear is really telling us:

Your fear doesn't mean: *"Stand still! Don't move! There is danger ahead."*

Your fear doesn't mean: *"Don't go forward until you know exactly what's going to happen."*

Your fear means: *"Get ready! Be prepared! A dream is trying to push its way out. Give it all the help you can."*

Your fear means: *"Here are the obstacles in your way. I'm showing them to you so you can get rid of them once and for all."*

Imagine that your dreams are like a flower bud pushing its way through the soil, trying to reach the air and the sunlight so it can blossom and grow. Fear is like the dirt that gets stirred up and shaken off when the flower breaks through that final barrier of earth. The presence of fear in your life means that your dreams are alive and well. Something wonderful is about to happen to you!

It's so important to know how to interpret these times when you feel overwhelmed by fear and to recognize them as the doorways to great transformation. For me, learning how to courageously stand in the center of the storm of my fear and not be seduced by its sound and fury has been an essential part of my spiritual progress.

I remember one time particularly, while attending a meditation retreat with my spiritual teacher, when she helped teach me this important lesson. It had been several months since I'd seen her, months during which I had worked very hard, completed many projects, and felt really good about myself. I was so excited to return back to where she was living and share the good news of my accomplishments. But within a few hours of arriving at the retreat site, I began to be assaulted by fears of every size and shape: fears about my career, my relationships, my spiritual development, my dreams, everything! It was as if all of my certainty about my life had vanished and been replaced by an unending supply of doubts. Suddenly, I felt like I was wandering through a dark, scary forest with no map.

Several days later at the end of a lecture, my teacher made time to greet each of her students one by one, something I normally looked forward to with great joy. As I waited for my turn, I was horrified to find that my fearful state was growing even worse. I had wanted to see her and share how well I was doing. Instead, I was a total wreck. All my confidence, all my clarity had vanished and as the line moved forward to where she was sitting, tears began to pour from my eyes. How could I face her in such a pitiful condition? I felt weak, as if somehow I had failed because I was so afraid.

Then it was my turn and I approached with folded hands in the traditional, respectful fashion, quickly nodded, and turned away, hoping to leave before she noticed my tear-stained face. Of course, in her amazing way, she noticed everything and said, "Barbara, what's going on?"

"Oh no," I thought to myself. "Now I have to confess how confused and afraid I am. What will she think of me?" So I took a deep breath and told her the whole story: how I had worked so hard for the past few months and had been feeling stable, peaceful, and confident; how I couldn't wait to come tell her so she would be proud of my efforts and my spiritual progress; and how, for the past week, it seemed everything had fallen apart and all I was feeling was fear about every aspect of my life.

"I wanted you to see me feeling strong and clear and together," I said in a trembling voice, "but instead, I'm so confused and afraid."

My teacher smiled at me, the most radiant, joyful smile drenched with delight and unconditional love, and responded, "Ahhhh, but I like this soooo much better." Then she squeezed my hand and turned to greet the next person in line.

I stumbled away in a daze, her words echoing in my mind: " 'But I like this so much better.' What did she mean? That she liked seeing me feeling so awful?" I knew that wasn't true. I was mystified by her message to me and determined to contemplate it until I discovered its deeper meaning, which I knew would be exactly what I needed to hear.

Later that day, I bumped into one of the senior meditation teachers at the retreat whom I admired very much and decided to get her opinion on what had transpired.

I carefully explained the events, and asked her what she thought that phrase meant.

"How fantastic!" this woman began. "She was really pleased with you."

"Pleased?" I asked with disbelief. "Why would she be pleased to see me feeling so frightened?"

"Because," the woman answered, "it means that you're making great progress. *That much fear is always a sign that you're moving very quickly. The faster you go, the more out of control you feel. And it's in that state of surrender that the real spiritual transformations can take place.*"

Suddenly, I understood and knew that what she was telling me was correct. I had been misinterpreting the fear as a sign that I was falling apart, when in fact it was a sign that I was approaching velocity speed and, as we've talked about in previous chapters, that I was opening myself up to really be worked on. I thought about what it would have been like if I'd approached my teacher feeling totally together, like I understood everything and had my life all in perfect order, and cringed—not a very humble attitude. Now I could see what she meant: she liked my vulnerability and my confusion so much better than my certainty because it opened me up to receiving more insight, more wisdom, more growth. She recognized my fear for what it was—my mind's natural response to a major shift in my consciousness. I was feeling disoriented because nothing looked like it used to look, a definite symptom of spiritual progress!

That evening, I wrote this entry in my journal:

> *If the scenery looks familiar, we know we haven't really traveled very far. But when we look around and think, "Where the hell am I?" then we know we have been moving very quickly and are making great progress along the path.*

This experience is one I return to over and over again whenever I am feeling fear, to remind myself that something profound is happening. Knowing the true nature of my fear helps to strengthen my courage and keep me focused on my true goal.

Making the Decision to Be Afraid or Not

> *If you are distressed by anything external,*
> *the pain is not due to the thing itself but*
> *to your own estimate of it;*
> *and this you have the power to revoke at any moment.*
> MARCUS AURELIUS

Here's another important lesson about fear:

> **Fear is not inherent in an experience;**
> **we bring our fear to the experience.**

Most experiences themselves are neither positive nor negative as we discussed earlier in this book—they're *neutral*. It's what we project on to them that makes them feel positive *or negative.* This principle is especially true when it comes to our fear, and understanding it is the key to conquering your fear.

For instance, if someone asked me to jump out of a plane with a parachute on my back, I'd be terrified. But a skydiver doing that same activity would probably not feel any fear at all—just excitement. On the other hand, if I asked the skydiver to give a talk without notes in front of three thousand people, she might be scared to death. I, on the other hand, would find that activity stimulating and fun. *The skydiving and the lecture in themselves don't contain the fear—each of us would bring the experience of fear to these events.*

**You are the one who decides
to bring your fear into the moment.
So since you choose what you are frightened about,
you can unchoose it.**

This is a very profound realization that can be the source of your courage. Every day you are choosing what to feel afraid of and what not to feel afraid of. You might perform three tasks that someone else would find frightening without even thinking about them and then worry about two others. For some reason, confronting one person in a difficult conversation scares you, while confronting another is no big deal. *It's your mind that is deciding what you're going to be scared of and what you won't be scared of.*

You choose what to be afraid of, so you can un-choose it. You decide whether it's a snake in the road or a rope. Naturally, this doesn't always apply to extreme situations, like having major surgery, or performing a death-defying act, yet even under these circumstances we will all have different reactions.

One way to pull yourself into the moment and consciously make a decision about which you want to make bigger, your courage or your fear, is to ask yourself the following question:

"Am I safe right now?"

Fear pulls us out of the moment, out of the now, and projects us into an imagined future in which we think harm will come to us. Think about it—*very few of the things you feel afraid of are actually happening to you while you are afraid—they are things you fear* might *happen to you in the future.*

> When you are feeling fear
> you are usually not in the moment,
> and when you are not in the moment,
> you are disconnected from your courage and
> your true self.

This question "Am I safe right now?" forces you into present time and helps you step back from your fear. Then you'll be able to reconnect with your visionary and find your courage again.

Having a Conversation with Your Fear

We started this chapter by talking about how you have a relationship with your fear. For some of us, the minute we hear the voice of fear, we drop everything and say, "Oh, come right on in and have a seat. I was about to do something I've been wanting to do, but I'll forget all about it if you think I should. Would you like to take over my mind for a while? It's fine with me. Nothing's more important than what you have to say."

This is like treating fear as an honored guest in your consciousness. I'd like to suggest something different—that you treat fear like a frightened child who has shown up at your door. Acknowledge it, talk with it, and find out where it has come from and what it is concerned about.

You'll notice that if you ask your fear to tell you what's bothering it, it will often start with the phrase: "What if . . ."

"What if I break up with my boyfriend, and I never find another one again for the rest of my life?

"What if I leave my present job and never find a new one?"

"What if I tell my mother that I don't like the way she treats me, and she never speaks to me again?"

"What if I open up a clothing store and I have no customers and end up going bankrupt?"

These "what ifs" terrorize us, immobilize us, and remove us from present time. You imagine that you are going to receive a negative result in the future from something you decide to do.

To help you overcome your fear of what might happen in the future, I suggest using a technique of talking to your fear which I call *running out your fear*. The technique is really very simple and, if you do it correctly, it's also a lot of fun! Here's how it works:

Imagine that I am talking to my friend Rebecca about her fear of not finding a new job in the field she wants to work in, and she asks me to help her talk through her fears. The first thing I say to Rebecca is:

"Tell me what you are afraid of."

Rebecca answers: "I'm afraid that if I quit my job before I have a new one, I may be out of a job for a while."

Next, I ask: **"And then what are you afraid will happen?"**

Rebecca: "And then I'll feel pressured to look for a new job."

"And then what?"

"And then maybe I will look and look, but will never find a job that I want."

"And then what?"

"And then I won't have money to pay my mortgage."

"And then what?"

"And then, I will have to sell my house."

"And then what?"

"And then, I'll have to move into a tiny apartment somewhere."

"And then what?"

"And then I'll have to get some menial job like waiting on tables or housecleaning to survive."

"And then what?"

"And then, I'll hate doing that so much and won't be able to continue, and won't have any job at all."

"And then what?"

"And then I'll never meet a man because my self-esteem will be so low and I'll be on welfare."

"And then what?"

"And then I won't have any money or a relationship and will be totally depressed and alone."

"And then what?"

"And then I'll probably get kicked out of my apartment and will end up on the streets, a bag lady."

"And then what?"

"And then, I'll just die, poor and alone, and no one will even know."

I'm sure you realize that at this point, Rebecca is laughing at herself. Somewhere during this process, she hears herself imagining the worst possible fears and knows that *there is no way she would allow these things to happen to her.* Maybe she would stay out of work for a few months, but she certainly wouldn't sit around and procrastinate if it meant losing her home or getting thrown out on the street. Although some people do allow themselves to end up in these sad situations, most of us stop this process way before it gets to the end.

This exercise gives you permission to run out your greatest fears, taking them to an extreme. The result: By verbalizing your feelings, you identify them as specific worries, not just vague, overwhelming thoughts of dread. Making your fear express itself out loud dissipates its energy and gives you more power over it.

In addition, as you hear yourself express these emotions, you reach a point at which you know there is no way you would allow this to happen to you. In that moment, your mind says, "Hey, I wouldn't stand for that happening to me." Suddenly, you are in control of your life again.

You can do this technique with a partner or friend or by yourself, either out loud or on paper. This is also a great technique to use with your children. Just say, "Let's play the 'And Then What' game." It's so important to give children permission to run out their fears. They love feeling safe enough to talk about them and it teaches how we have the choice to use our thoughts as our enemy or as our friend.

Learning to Live with Your Fear, But Not As Your Fear

I was giving a lecture to a large group of people a few months ago and toward the end, a woman about my age stood up to ask a question.

"Barbara," she began in a very timid voice, "I admire you so much. Could you tell me how you got rid of all of your fears of failure to become the success you are today?"

When I heard this question, I laughed, not at the woman, but at her flattering but incorrect assumption that I didn't have any fears. "I'm going to give you the answer you may not be expecting," I responded. "I didn't get rid of my fears. In fact, I have more fear now than I did when I began my career twenty years ago! Then, I was taking little risks—giving a lecture to fifteen people, writing a brochure, talking to one person about his problems. But now I'm taking enormous risks—giving a lecture to three thousand people, going on TV and sharing my ideas with twenty million viewers, writing a book and hoping people will like it. *Since the risks are bigger, so are my fears.*"

The woman in the audience looked shocked. "But how come you appear so confident?" she asked.

"I'm confident *not* that I can eliminate my fears, but that I can act *in spite* of them." I answered.

> Freedom doesn't mean having no fear.
> It means acting in spite of your fear.

Each time I set out to do something I haven't done before, I feel nervous and a little afraid. I can remember the first seminar I gave, the first local TV show I did, the first national TV show I appeared on, the first conference I spoke at, the first time I met with a publisher, the first book tour I went on, the first news report I wrote. Each time I was fearful because I was experiencing something new and was venturing out of my comfort zone. And each time after I'd completed whatever it was that I was doing, the fear magically disappeared. I didn't start out with confidence—finding the courage to do what I was frightened of, over and over again, is what gave me confidence.

This is one of the most important messages of Secret Number Six:

> **If you wait for your fear to go away**
> **before you do something new or challenging,**
> **you will wait forever.**

Many of us have the mistaken notion that one day we will wake up, check inside of ourselves, and discover that miraculously our fear is gone and then we'll finally be free to write our books/change our jobs/have that difficult conversation with our mates/go back to school or whatever it is we were afraid to do. Fear doesn't just go away, especially before you do something new. Of course you're going to be nervous—you've never done it before. *In fact, fear doesn't leave while you're in a human body. It is a natural response the body and mind have to certain experiences.* So waiting for it to disappear before fully living your life makes no sense. I love this quote by Sydney J. Harris:

> *Regret for the things we did can be tempered by time;*
> *it is regret for the things we did not do that is*
> *inconsolable.*

I am not advocating being foolhardy or doing things that are "risky," like betting all of your money on a horse race or trying to ski down a mountain for the first time with no lessons, all in the name of not waiting for your fear to go away. *I'm talking about beginning to take the risks you know you need to take to make your dreams come true by making your courage bigger than your fear.* Does this mean you have to go out there and rearrange your entire life tomorrow, facing every single challenge you have been putting off? Not at all! In fact, some leaps don't look like leaps at all, but are the product of having taken one small step after the other. You progress one inch at a time and before you know it, you have traveled miles and miles toward your goal. "The distance is nothing," a great French philosopher once said, "it is only the first step that is difficult."

Remember:
You may not get to choose whether or not you feel fear,
but you do get to choose
whether you want to *identify* with the fear,
or whether you want to *witness* the fear.

You can apply the witnessing techniques from Secret Number Five about the mind to the emotion of fear, as well. Whenever you're feeling afraid, say to yourself:

I have fear, but I am *not* my fear.
I am that which is *noticing* the fear.

This is a wonderful mantra to repeat when you're having fearful thoughts. Think it quietly to yourself over and over or say it out loud if you wish. I use this fear mantra frequently, and I notice that within a few minutes of focusing on it I begin to feel much more detached from the fear, and free from the emotional and physiological effects it was having on me.

Starving Your Fear and Feeding Your Courage

There are some simple changes you can make in your life that will help you feel less fear and experience more courage. I've made a list of several things that can help you strengthen your visionary and feed your courage, and some other things to avoid because if you don't, they will feed your fear. Living with courage means "starving" your fear by eliminating all of the conditions in the left column, and "feeding" your visionary by creating the conditions in the right column.

WHAT FEEDS YOUR FEAR	WHAT FEEDS YOUR VISIONARY
Judgment	*Love*
Isolation from Other People	*Support from Other People*
Fatigue	*Rest*

Mental Disorganization and Confusion	*Clear Goals and Plans*
Physical Disorderliness and Chaos	*Orderliness and Cleanliness*
Spending Time with Negative People	*Spending Time with Positive People*
Drugs and Alcohol	*Being Out in Nature*
Poor Diet—Sugar, Junk Food, etc.	*Eating a Healthy and Balanced Diet*
Watching Too Much TV, Particularly Violence and Drama	*Reading Inspirational Books, Listening to Motivational Tapes*
Depriving Yourself	*Rewarding Yourself*
Holding in Feelings	*Sharing Feelings*
Closed-Minded Environments in Which Change Is Resisted	*Conscious Environments in Which Change is Encouraged*

You may want to add to this list based on your own experience. The more conscious you become of what you can do to feed your visionary and tap into your natural courage, and what you can avoid to starve your fear, the more powerful and free you'll begin to feel.

Courage is a form of love.
It is a way to love yourself
and honor the truth about who you really are.

When I first began my spiritual journey many years ago, I read the *Dune* series, the wonderful science fiction novels by Frank Herbert. These fascinating books chronicle the history of an imaginary desert planet called Arrakis and its inhabitants, many of whom are seeking to experience life's greatest inner mysteries. On this planet, there is a spiritual order called the Bene Gesserit, an ancient school of mental and physical training established primarily for female students who attain high states of consciousness and mystical powers.

I remember the excitement I felt when I first read *Dune*, entering a world in which the secret spiritual power and training was the domain of women. I longed to be a member of the Bene Gesserit and to undergo the many stages of training the initiates experience until they achieve perfect freedom. There was a credo, a sort of mantra, that these women used in their efforts to master their minds and particularly, the fears that would rob them of their natural intuition and wisdom:

> *I must not fear. Fear is the mind-killer. Fear is the little death that brings total obliteration. I will face my fear. I will permit it to pass over me and through me. And when it has gone past I will turn the inner eye to see its path. Where the fear has gone there will be nothing. Only I will remain.*

I got chills when I first read these words. They spoke to something deep within my soul, a truth that I had forgotten but which had not died, the truth that I was not my fear, that I, too, was something magical, ancient, and unchanging. I typed the words out onto a small piece of paper and taped it on my mirror where I could see it every day. Soon after, I began my formal spiritual studies and practices, not unlike that ancient school I'd longed to be a part of.

How many times over the past thirty years have I read this credo to myself? Times when I was feeling so much fear, I could hardly breathe. Times when my dreams had been shattered yet again and I was afraid I would never find my way back to simple happiness. Times when it seemed that all my efforts to share my message with others were being thwarted by dark forces that wanted me to give up. Times when I just didn't know if I had enough courage to face the steep and seemingly unconquerable mountain before me.

I moved this paper from my first typewriter to my second to my first computer to the next, from one apartment to my first house to the next. I wrote every one of my books looking at it taped to the bottom of my computer screen. I am looking at it right now.

Where the fear has gone there will be nothing. Only I will remain.

Fears have come and fears have gone, but I am still here. My vision, my courage, my love. Only that remains.

Know that your fears, too, will come and go.
Let them pass over you and through you.
Then, turn your vision within,
and you will see the truth:
Only you will remain . . .

You Must Love
Yourself Before
You Can Truly
Give Love
or Receive Love
from Anyone Else

*To love oneself is the beginning
of a life-long romance.*

OSCAR WILDE

From the day we are born until the day we die, we seek out love in countless ways. Sometimes our search for love is as obvious as opening our arms and pulling our lover close to us; sometimes it is as subtle as the brief smile we offer to a stranger as we pass each other in a doorway. Sometimes we run after love, certain that we cannot live without it; sometimes we hide from love, secretly hoping it will run after us. Sometimes the love we find lasts a lifetime; sometimes it awakens just for an instant and then vanishes.

I have spent most of my life as a student and teacher of love and my own search for it has been passionate, dramatic, relentless, and enlightening. This path has led me, finally and irrevocably, to one simple yet profound conclusion: Ultimately, even our search for love must direct us within, to what the ancients call our true self, as we discover a very real and fulfilling relationship with *our own inner companion.*

The most important relationship you ever have is with yourself.
The most important relationship you need to heal is with yourself.
The person you need to truly fall in love with is yourself.

For most of my life, this was just an inspiring, uplifting concept—that I should love myself. I believed it. I gave this advice to my friends and my students. I tried my best to put this principle into practice. But deep inside, I never really felt I could experience the intense love I felt for others with and for my own self.

And then, something happened to me that changed my understanding of love forever.

It Was Always Only My Own Love

Some people might think it is ironic that one of the most profound love stories of my life appears to contains heartbreak, rejection, and betrayal. Yet it is this very story from my past that I want to share with you, for out of it emerged wisdom I could not have achieved in any other way.

All love stories begin happily and mine was no exception. I had grown very close to a man I'd known for some time, someone for whom I had great respect and admiration. He was brilliant, charming, and dedicated to his own spiritual pursuits. I had never been with anyone like him and it seemed as if he was the fulfillment of so many secret wishes I'd had about the kind of person with whom I could have a truly conscious and emotionally elevated relationship.

I could hardly believe I'd finally met someone who appeared to appreciate all the different parts of me, parts that had never been fully accepted by anyone. I was so much in love, love unlike anything I'd ever experienced. I would sit for hours feeling waves and waves of ecstasy. And with each visit, each phone call, each letter, I would get higher and higher.

Then, things began to go wrong and my dream of finding a soul mate turned into a horrific nightmare unlike anything I'd ever experienced. I will spare you the painful details of how the drama unfolded, but the result was that this man began a relationship with someone else without even telling me about it. Soon thereafter, I discovered that during our time together he'd been involved with at least one other woman, possibly more, even sending us the same love letters, word for word.

Basically, I just fell apart. I felt shocked, heartbroken, devastated, deceived, and used. Day after day, I would lie on my bed and sob until I passed out from exhaustion. This was certainly not the first time in my life a man had hurt me or left me. But it was the first time I'd ever been lied to in this way, the first time I'd ever felt so deeply betrayed. *I wasn't just mourning for what I had lost, but for what I now knew I'd actually never had in the first place.*

As the weeks passed, my mind moved from pure disbelief into a desperate need to understand what had happened. I began to go over and over every moment of the relationship, searching for some clue that might enlighten me, that might help me make sense of all that had taken place. I sorted through now-painful memories of times I'd spent with this man in which I'd felt so much love, conversations we'd had during which I'd felt so much connection. Had I been deluding myself completely, living in a total dream world, making up the emotions I thought I was experiencing? I knew this wasn't true, that I *had* felt love, I *had* felt joy, I *had* felt ecstasy. At the time, I'd been sure that he was feeling that same love. Of course, now I knew that wasn't the case.

The more I analyzed the situation, the more confused I became. All along, I'd been thinking that this man was giving me intense love, profound intimacy. Obviously, he hadn't been giving me anything of the sort. In fact, he hadn't even really been there at all. So I asked myself, "Barbara, if he wasn't actually giving you that love, then where was that love you were feeling coming from?"

Suddenly, it was as if my mind cleared and I was struck with an astonishing revelation:

The love I'd been feeling had come from inside of me.

When I'd felt all that love, whose love was I feeling? Mine. Whose joy was I feeling? Mine. Whose ecstasy was I feeling? Mine.

I wasn't feeling his love, because it hadn't existed in the way I thought it did. I wasn't feeling loved *by* him, because he wasn't loving me in the way I thought he was. *It was all my own love!*

My mind had *assigned* my love to this person, *as if he was the source of it*. But as I discovered, he *wasn't* the source of it. In fact, he was hardly participating in the process at all. I was the source of the love I was feeling.

> Love doesn't come from the outside of your life in.
> Love comes from the inside out.

Now another outrageous revelation exploded in my consciousness:

If I was the source of my love for him, then I've always been the source of all the love I've ever felt.

I began to look back on every relationship I'd ever had. Whether they'd turned out horribly or turned out wonderfully, weren't the mechanics the same as they'd been in this one? *Who had ever given me any love? Wasn't it always my own love that I was feeling?* I would meet someone and he would do the right things or say the right things that gave my mind "permission" to decide I loved him. Then, I would start feeling all this love. But the other person hadn't actually given me anything. *I had simply decided to allow myself to feel that love.*

> You are the source of your own love.
> You decide when you're allowed to feel it
> and when you're not.
> But the love you feel is always yours.
> No one can give you any love you don't already have.

Then another profound realization hit me: If this person had never been the source of the love I felt, then when he decided to leave my life, what had I truly lost? *Nothing.* Was I less lovable because he was no longer in my life? Did I have less love inside of me? No. So what was different? He had stopped doing certain things or saying certain things that had given me permission to feel the love and I had concluded: "I don't feel loved by him anymore." Actually, I wasn't *allowing* myself to feel my own love anymore. I had decided to stop experiencing all that love because he wasn't around to bounce it off of, to focus it on. *I was the one who was taking the experience of love away from myself!*

This was so clear because of the painful situation I'd just gone through, since this man hadn't taken anything away from me that I'd ever had in the first place. I was the one who decided I was lovable when I thought he was loving me, so I allowed myself to feel happy and in love. Then, he was gone and I concluded that I must be unlovable and decided to not allow myself to feel happy and in love. But nothing had really changed—it was all a game my own mind was playing with itself.

> No one gives you love,
> so no one can take love away from you.

I can still remember so clearly how I felt during this great awakening. I was sitting on my bed, joy bubbling up from deep within me. It was as if a veil of ignorance had just been lifted from my eyes and I could see the truth clearly for the first time. I recall saying to myself, "Well, if this is all true and it's always been your own love, why don't you try to feel it right now?"

I closed my eyes, took some long, deep breaths, and thought about all of the people I'd loved intimately in my life. Some I was still close with. Some I hadn't seen in years. Some had chosen to leave me. Some I had left. All of a sudden, I felt waves of beautiful love, ecstatic love, delicious love begin to wash over me. I allowed myself to feel the love without trying to assign it to any one person or give it any meaning. And as I did, the love grew stronger and more intense until I felt as if I was one huge, pulsating ocean of love. Tears of happiness trickled down my cheeks as I floated in this blissful sensation. And I had the thought:

"This is what it means to be *in* love."

Suddenly, I felt free in a way that I'd never felt free before. *For the first time in my life, I realized I was in love—not with anyone, just in the state of love.* I recognized this feeling. I'd had it many times before, but had always assumed it was because of how someone else was loving me. But here I was sitting alone on my bed, not in a relationship with anyone, and I was totally, wildly, ecstatically in love. I was embraced by my own love. *I had finally found my true inner companion.*

This experience provided me with one of the most powerful turning points of my life. I have never experienced love in the same way again. Many of the lessons and realizations form the basis of this chapter and I am certain that without having gone through that agonizing relationship, I wouldn't have experienced such a dramatic and permanent awakening. Now when I look back, I feel such gratitude toward this man, who, by misleading me and breaking my heart, unwittingly taught me more about true love than I ever could have learned if we'd lived happily ever after.

No One Can Give You Any More Love Than You Already Have

You don't have to go through the excruciatingly painful kind of experience I did to have these same revelations for yourself. Just think about your own love history and you'll discover that these principles are true for you, as well. For instance, have you ever thought everything was fine in a relationship, only to have a partner confess that he or she had been upset with you, or unhappy about something for a while? When you didn't know that they were feeling this way yet, you were walking around happy and in love. The truth is, this person was already not loving you as much, but since you weren't aware of it, you were still giving yourself permission to feel the love. You weren't in love because he or she was loving you. You were in love because you gave yourself permission to be in love.

Here's another example: Imagine you have a partner right now and he does something to show you his love— he puts his arm around you, or kisses you and says something sweet, or gives you a thoughtful gift. You feel this rush of love rise up in your heart, right? Ask yourself: Did he just *give* you anything? Was it as if you got an injection of love into your body? Did he take a jug of love, open your mouth, and pour it down your throat? Did he add something like a chip in your brain that made you feel loved? Is there something physically in you that wasn't in you before? Did he put love inside of you? What did that person actually give you? Nothing.

So why are you feeling more love in that moment? *Because he did something that you are using as an opportunity to feel more of your own love that's always been there.* Your love has been sitting inside of you like an ocean. And in that moment, it has decided to rise up in waves. But nothing he did actually added to the volume of your love.

No one can ever add to your love,
and no one can ever subtract from your love.
You already have an infinite supply.

Here is the seventh principle:

> **SECRET NUMBER SEVEN:**
>
> **YOU MUST LOVE YOURSELF
> BEFORE YOU CAN REALLY GIVE
> LOVE OR RECEIVE LOVE
> FROM ANYONE ELSE**

You must find your own inner love, your own inner companion, before you can even experience love in anyone else's presence. And the good news is that that love *is* there within you. It is your greatest treasure. This is what all the saints and sages meant when they said, "God dwells within you as you," or "You are love." Your love is that kingdom of heaven inside that the Bible tells us to seek first, promising that then everything else will come to us.

How You Give Other People Credit for Your Own Love

One of the first steps in learning to love yourself is recognizing how you may be giving other people credit for the love you are feeling, rather than realizing it is your own love. This is one of the many remarkable insights I had as a part of the whole story I've shared with you—*that in relationships, I would feel my own love, my own joy, my own enthusiasm, and assign that experience to the person I was with, as if he was the source of it.*

For instance, I would be taking a walk on the beach with my partner, gazing out at the beautiful turquoise ocean, inhaling the fresh, salty breeze, feeling the kiss of the sun's warmth on my skin. Joy and love would rise up within my heart. I would feel so happy, so full of love. And I would turn to my mate and say, "You are so wonderful. I love you. I love being here with you. You make me so happy."

What was I really feeling in that moment? I was feeling my own love, my own joy, my own gratitude for life. Was my mate "making" me happy, making me feel loved? No—*I was assigning my own feeling of happiness and love to him.* It's not that I didn't adore being there with him, that it didn't add to my fulfillment, *but the source of the love was within me.*

When I began reflecting on my own relationships from this point of view, I asked myself an interesting question:

"What does it take for me to assign my love to another person?"

In other words, what conditions have I decided are necessary in order for me to feel "in love"? Does the person have to look a certain way? Behave a certain way? Possess certain characteristics that "qualify" him? What if one of these is missing? Will it be impossible for me to feel "in love," even though that same love is sitting there inside of me?

We all have secret mental lists of what qualities are necessary for us to assign our experience of love to others. The problem with this is that it gives the other person the responsibility for making you feel in love, making you feel happy from moment to moment. This is why you get angry at your partner when he does things you don't like: he is taking away your excuse to love him! "I was enjoying loving him so much," your mind thinks with a sigh. "But he just said something really stupid and now I can't feel the love anymore—at least not until he says or does something that gives me an excuse to feel the love again."

Think about it: If all you are ever experiencing is your own love, then it seems pretty arbitrary that your mind has concluded you can't feel love if your mate says or does certain things. I'm not saying you should like everything a partner does, but to turn the love off and on because he didn't fulfill your expectations is just a game your mind is playing with itself. "I will let my own love rise up under these conditions, but not under these."

We can take this one step further: If you're single, you may believe that you can't fall in love with someone who's forty pounds overweight, or doesn't have the kind of job you think he should, or who is interested in something you find boring, or whatever traits you've decided disqualify him. But those are just conditions your mind has decided must be present for you to let your own love flow. This is a way you may be cutting yourself off from the possibility of finding a truly divine relationship.

Give Yourself Permission to Be In Love All the Time

The truth is, we are all capable of experiencing love with so many more people than we believe we could. In fact, if we had an enlightened mind and totally open heart, we could experience the fullness of our own love in the presence of anyone. This has been the experience of great saints and masters throughout the ages. They live in the state of love, in the state of their own fullness, and they experience that love no matter who they are with.

Most of us believe that we need to be in an intimate relationship before we can be "in love." We think another person is necessary! In fact, the opposite is true:

Learning how to be "in love" by ourselves,
with ourselves,
will allow us to experience true love for the first time.
You have to be in the state of love
before you can have any kind of meaningful
relationship.

If you wait to connect with your inner love, if you wait to be *in love* until you meet a special someone, you're going to be in trouble. Why? Because if you're not *in love* and he's not *in love* and you're each hoping the other person will make you feel *in love*, you'll end up disappointed and resentful.

No one can give you love you're not already feeling. No one can fill you with anything you don't already possess. You should be in love before you leave the house, before you go out on a date, or if you're already with a mate, before you spend time together. Then, when someone who is also in love meets you or sees you, you can be in love together! Side by side, you can celebrate the miracle of the love that is dancing within you and between you. As the great mystical Sufi poet Rumi says so beautifully:

The minute I heard my first love story
I started looking for you, not knowing
how blind that was.
Lovers don't finally meet somewhere.
They're in each other all along.

This is an enlightened relationship. Love is never actually exchanged—you don't give it and your partner doesn't receive it. *Rather, both of you agree to feel your own love at the same time.* And that love resonates back and forth like a joyous bridge connecting your two hearts.

Love isn't something we can actually get
from anyone else—
it's a state that we are either in
or one that we aren't in.

When you begin to have this kind of inner relationship with yourself, you realize that being "in love" is a state that you can experience no matter what's happening around you. If someone is there to be in love with, that's great. And if you're alone, you can still be in love. And if you have a partner but he is in a bad mood, or not feeling his own love, you can still feel your own love, enjoy your own love. *You are the source of your love.*

Really beginning to love yourself
means giving yourself permission
to feel your own love, to be "in" your own love.

More and more in my own life, I've been experiencing being in love in every moment. I have so much love inside of me and the task is for me to immerse myself in it, just as I would immerse myself in the ocean for a swim, and then interact with people from that state of love. Being "in love" is a conscious decision I make—*I give myself permission to feel my own love in someone else's presence.*

Walking around in love, I get to have dozens of mini "love affairs" every day. I stop at the local cafe in town for some coffee, and as the girl takes my order, I allow myself to look deeply into her eyes, to let her see the depth of the love inside of me, to rejoice in her uniqueness, to feel her, and for a moment we smile, connect, and I am in love. I go to an appointment and as I leave my car with the parking attendant, I pause for a moment and find my own love, handing the valet the keys and chatting briefly with him about the weather as if he is my most intimate friend. I sit in a meeting with several people I've never met before, feeling the love pulsating inside me, and imagining I am surrounded by my most dear ones.

You Don't Need Someone Else's Permission to Love Them

Sometimes I get so high doing this that I am sure I must look intoxicated. Recently, I took a trip to the beautiful Florida Keys with two very dear male friends. I could never be involved with either of these men romantically for many reasons, and they are like brothers to me. Ten years ago, if I'd gone to a beautiful vacation spot without a lover, I would have spent my days wishing I'd been there with someone with whom I was in love instead of just with friends. But on this trip, I did no such thing, for I *was* in love. I gave myself permission to feel all of my own love and to enjoy it in their presence, and they did the same. The result was that we were in a perpetual state of bliss for days on end.

One night we went to a local restaurant right on the beach for dinner. We sat at the table under the stars, gazing into one another's eyes with such delight, laughing, and feeling so grateful to be alive. At one point I got up to find the restroom and as I passed our waitress, she smiled at me and said, "I have to tell you that I am really having a great time watching you. You look like you are so much in love. I just can't figure out which one of those guys you're in love with, or if it's both!"

I smiled back, letting her, too, feel all of my love in that moment and gave the only honest answer I could: "It's both!"

She looked at me and for a moment her eyes were wide with surprise, and I wondered if I'd shocked her. Then, her face lit up with an enormous grin and she said, "You go, girl!"

Learning to be in the state of your own love isn't difficult at all. It's a matter of *noticing when you're feel-*

ing love and following the sensation back to its source inside of you. Let's say that you see somebody you love today or tomorrow and in his or her presence you feel that rush of emotion in your heart, that feeling called love. When you become aware of the love, instead of thinking it's coming from the other person, point out to yourself that it's coming from inside of you. Identify the love as yours.

You might want to ask yourself:

"Whose love am I feeling?"

or,

"Where is the source of this love?"

Perhaps you are giving one of your children a good-bye hug before school and you notice that your heart is swelling with love. Say to yourself: *"I am feeling my own love."* Perhaps you are driving to work and notice how beautiful someone's garden looks and feel a wave of delight pass through you. Say to yourself, *"I am feeling my own love."* Perhaps you are wrapped in an intimate embrace with your lover and your body is melting with pleasure. Remind yourself, *"This is my love."*

Whenever you're feeling any joy,
whenever you feel any happiness,
whenever you feel any love or goodness in your heart,
honor it as your own love,
as God's love inside of you.
Then you will start loving yourself.
You'll start seeing that who you are is love.

Your Love Helps Others Love Themselves

Sometimes we feel reticent to love ourselves this much, fearing that we will somehow be vain or that we will be taking away our love from others. Actually, the opposite is true. *When you love yourself, you give other people permission to love themselves, as well.*

Recently a friend of mine from New Zealand stayed with me for a month. This woman is like a sister to me and we lived together harmoniously, grateful for each other's company. The day before she left, she said something that touched my heart so deeply.

"It's been amazing to watch you for all these weeks, Barbara," she began. "You've never criticized me once for anything I've done or said. You haven't had one judgment of me during my entire visit. You are always saying kind and caring things to me. I haven't heard one negative comment come out of your mouth. And I realize that you can treat me this way because it is the way you treat yourself—with love and respect." She paused and her eyes filled with tears. "I've never had a friend treat me with so much love."

I was so moved by what my friend shared with me and as I thought about her words, I realized that she was right—*the more I was learning to love myself, the more I naturally could feel and express genuine love for others, without even having to make a conscious effort.* I recalled something someone once wrote about my spiritual teacher: "She loves herself so much that it's hard not to like yourself in her presence."

This is true for all great beings. They reverberate with so much love that in their presence, we start to feel good about ourselves. We start to feel we want to treat ourselves with more respect. We begin to get in touch with our own love.

I was happy hearing my friend's gratitude that my practice of honoring my own love was allowing me to radiate more love to others. This is the real gift we can all give to the people we care about, our mates, our friends, our children—to love ourselves so much that the waves of our own joy splash onto them.

When you know how to fill yourself up from the inside out,
you are able to enter into your outer relationships
with a full heart and self-born contentment
that others will feel and respond to.

You Never Really Give Anyone Else Your Love

Secret Number Seven tells us that we must love ourselves first before we can give or receive love. But what happens to people who don't love themselves, who try to get love from the outside in, rather than from the inside out?

Have you ever tried to love somebody who did not want to receive your love or who was afraid to open up? You give and you give and you give, pouring your heart and soul into the relationship, but it's as if he is impervious to all you're offering. Perhaps years go by, and at the end, it seems like he didn't absorb one drop of your love, as if it drained right through him onto the floor. At the end of this type of relationship, you feel emotionally exhausted and your mate walks away as if he didn't feel any more love in his heart than on day one. *And you feel like a failure because your love didn't make a difference.*

Your love cannot do anything but be an excuse for someone else to feel the love he already has for himself. Remember: You can't ever give anybody love they are not already feeling, no matter how hard you try.

> You can't really make another person feel loved.
> If he isn't capable of loving himself in the first place,
> he's not going to feel loved by you, either.

Many years ago, I was in a relationship with a man who had been very emotionally wounded in childhood and deep inside felt like an impostor, like he wasn't good enough. He was intelligent and talented, but never seemed to get his life together or to achieve any kind of stability or success. We shared a very deep connection and I felt great love for him. And yes, I confess, I wanted to *help* him.

It soon became apparent that our relationship was one big power struggle—I would try to love him and he would push my love away. I would try to support him and he would sabotage my efforts. I would lend him money to pay off his debts and he would get into more debt. I would create an opportunity for him to work and he would somehow undermine my efforts. I remember dozens of times, sitting in front of him, tears streaming down my face, pleading with him to let my love in, to be good to himself, to take positive action in his life, only to have him stare back at me, frozen and unable to respond.

Finally, I knew it had to end. The relationship was draining me and getting worse every day. We went through the inevitable, terrible confrontation, the drama, and the moving out.

One night, alone in my house, I found myself sobbing uncontrollably in my bedroom as I thought about my former mate. I felt overcome by grief, grief I couldn't really understand, since I was relieved to be on my own again. Suddenly, it hit me: *I was crying because I felt my love hadn't healed this person I cared for. I was crying because I hadn't been able to fill his heart. I was crying because I felt I had failed.*

I called a very wise friend and poured my heart out. He listened patiently to my tears, my frustrations. At one point, I shared how much it hurt me that this man I'd loved so deeply had spent most of our relationship angry at me. "Why was he so angry?" I wept. "All I did was love him."

"Don't you see why he was angry, Barbara?" my friend answered softly. "You loved him more than he loves himself."

All at once, I understood. My love for my partner had made him feel inadequate. I saw things in him he couldn't live up to, couldn't see in himself. My love became a reminder of his failure to love himself and he ended up resenting me for the very love he wanted so desperately.

Of course, I was destined to fail. He didn't love himself and no matter how much of my own love I felt in his presence, no matter how much I could see the love inside of him, it made no difference. Nothing I did could make a difference.

I worked very hard for the next few months to forgive myself for thinking I had failed this man by not getting him to love himself more. Perhaps there is someone in your own life you've been feeling guilty about not getting through to, someone you wanted to fill up with your love but couldn't. Release that burden of responsibility you've been carrying. Just let it go. You didn't fail. That person just couldn't enjoy your love because he wasn't enjoying his own.

We think our love can leave our hearts and go into people, like a transfusion that will give them new life, but it can't. *Your love can call out to someone else's love and wake it from a deep sleep, but it can't actually be exchanged and fill someone's emptiness.* And of course the same is true for their love—no one is going to fill you up. You need to find your own love inside.

Don't Postpone Loving Yourself

Years ago when I first began my personal growth work, I used to think I loved myself. I could point to times when I had treated myself very well or rewarded myself for an accomplishment; I could tell you about how I pampered myself with bubble baths or took myself out for a shopping spree. But as I looked more closely at my relationship with myself, I realized to my great dismay that my love for Barbara was very conditional.

Yes, I loved myself when my books sold well, or when I did a good job on a project, or when my relationship was going fine, or when I did what I thought I was supposed to, or achieved what I thought I should. But when I was frightened, I didn't love myself. When I was confused, I didn't love myself. When I was needy, I didn't love myself.

Most of us treat ourselves in the same way. We have a secret list in our minds that starts out: *I will love myself when . . .* and it's filled with conditions we've decided we must fulfill to qualify for our love.

> *I will love myself when I am the perfect weight.*
> *I will love myself when I find a boyfriend.*
> *I will love myself when I pay off all my debts.*
> *I will love myself when my kids do well in school and I feel I'm a successful parent.*
> *I will love myself when my husband finally opens up.*
> *I will love myself when I am getting along with everyone and no one dislikes me.*
> *I will love myself when I never have bad days.*
> *I will love myself when I never feel overwhelmed.*

This is actually a great exercise to do. Make a list of your secret conditions for loving yourself. You'll be shocked at how many there are and how impossible it would be to meet them. No wonder you find it difficult to get in touch with your own love every day—you're flunking your own unconscious tests!

**When you love yourself conditionally,
you cut yourself off from your own love inside.**

Loving yourself means loving yourself as you are. It means accepting yourself in your pleasure and your pain, your terror and your triumph. It means being tender toward yourself, never punishing yourself for how you are feeling. It means just letting yourself be and knowing when you do, you will move through whatever you are experiencing that much more quickly.

Loving yourself means honoring yourself for your courage on the path of growth. Honor yourself for how hard you've been working on yourself. Honor yourself for all the progress that you've made. Honor yourself for reading a book like this one and for all the other steps you've taken to become a more conscious, loving human being. Honor yourself for even knowing the places you're still stuck, for being honest about them, and not giving up. Honor yourself for every step you take.

We grow through being loved. When you were a child learning to walk, you took your first wobbly step and then fell to the ground. Your mother instinctively knew what to say: "Good girl! You took a step! I'm so proud of you! You are so wonderful!" And even though you fell down, and even though it hurt a little bit, you looked up at your mother's face, gazing at you with so much confidence and so much love, and you pulled yourself up and tried again.

Can you imagine what would have happened if, when you took your first step and fell, she had said, "What a klutz! One step—is that all you can do? Let's see you go back and forth across the room three times, then maybe I'll be impressed"? With this kind of feedback, you would have never learned to walk.

Love yourself for every step you are taking. Love yourself when you fall down and love yourself when you pick yourself back up again. Talk to yourself and say all the things you would want someone else to say to you. If you can't say them now to your own heart, you won't hear them even when someone else comes along.

Every day, I talk to myself with love. I use the most endearing terms I can think of. I speak to myself as if I am my own beloved. Just last night, as I was struggling with a part of this chapter, I took a break, got into the bathtub, and began talking to myself out loud: "Darling, you are doing such a wonderful job. I know you are tired, but you are almost done. And you're going to do it! I love you and I am proud of you. What a great accomplishment this will be. And you're being so honest, and so vulnerable, and so courageous! You're doing great, sweetheart, you really are."

"She talks to herself that way?" you may be thinking. The answer is: Yes, I do. And so should you. Don't you wish someone else would say those things to you? So why not say them to yourself? Your words and thoughts are powerful, as we saw earlier in the book. Every one counts. So make your words to yourself sweet and loving. Become your own beloved.

Love That No One Can Ever Take Away

When you discover your own inexhaustible love inside, you will begin to experience a freedom that can never be taken away from you. It is the freedom to be in love regardless of the circumstances of your life. It is the freedom to drink your own love, to taste its sweetness, to celebrate the miracle of its presence in your heart.

Recently I found this beautiful poem by Derek Walcott. It celebrates this reunion with yourself that we've been speaking about.

The time will come
when, with elation,
you will greet yourself arriving
at your own door, in your own mirror,
and each will smile at the other's welcome,

and say, sit here. Eat.
You will love again the stranger who was your self.
Give wine. Give bread. Give back your heart
to itself, to the stranger who has loved you

all your life, whom you ignored
for another, who knows you by heart.
Take down the love letters from the bookshelf,

the photographs, the desperate notes,
peel your own image from the mirror.
Sit. Feast on your life.

This morning, knowing I was about to finish this chapter, I went into meditation and asked if there was anything else I needed to share with you. Immediately, words began to emerge from the stillness and I wrote them down. I offer them as a message from my inner self that is love to your inner self that is love:

Love that is truly free, that stays with you, that no
*   one can take away, emerges from your own self.*
Invite others to enter into that state of your own love.
Do not seek their love.
You are the source of the love.

Someone may come to swim in your ocean, but
*   remember, it's your water.*

Love yourself.
Love yourself for where you've come from and how
*   you've arrived here.*
Love yourself for where you are.

And when you leave here, love yourself for the process of moving forward.

No matter what happens, just love yourself while it is happening.
This is the way to honor the truth of who you really are.
You are love.
You are love.
You are love.

All Relationships Are Your Mirrors and All People Are Your Teachers

The world is nothing but a school of love;
our relationships with our husband or wife,
with our children and parents,
with our friends and relatives are the university
in which we are meant to learn
what love and devotion truly are.

SWAMI MUKTANANDA

I'd like to take you on an imaginary journey: We are going to travel to a time before this life, when you were preparing to come back to earth. You are sitting in a large room with many other beings, all of whom are also waiting to return to this plane of existence in order to continue their growth as a soul. Each of you has been examining your previous life, noting the lessons you learned, as well as the lessons you still need to learn, the emotional skills you've mastered, as well as the ones you haven't quite gotten down yet. You are evaluating yourself with compassion, objectivity, and love. Nothing you see is viewed as good or bad—it's just where you are on your spiritual journey.

Wise teachers are present to assist you in understanding some of the more complex issues you still have left to face. With their help, you formulate a list of experiences you agree to undergo in this next incarnation as a human being. These experiences will be designed to present the perfect opportunities for you to grow into a more advanced and free soul.

Now, one of these ancient teachers addresses the group. "Are you ready?" she asks. All the souls gathered there nod in agreement. "Wonderful," she says with a radiant smile. "Let the selection process begin."

Someone stands up and begins to speak. "Greetings, friends. I spent my last lifetime in very selfish pursuits and I am determined not to do it again this next time. So I need to undergo the challenge of loving someone unconditionally—maybe someone who's going to be physically not well, or has some kind of problem I will have to tolerate. This will teach me selflessness and service. Does anyone qualify for this position?"

Another being stands. "Yes, I do! In fact, that would be perfect for me, as well. I spent my last lifetime obsessed with my physical beauty and athletic strength and forgot completely about my inner development. I've decided this time I must have no distractions from my spiritual growth and that I need to learn to love myself for who I am on the inside. So I'm going to have an accident in my thirties that leaves me partially disabled. It's a big commitment, but I'm ready for it. Do you think we could team up?"

"That would be wonderful," the first being responds with excitement. "What if we meet and get married before the accident and then I will have to take care of you for the rest of your life?"

"Oh, this is better than I'd hoped," the second being answers. "Because my other big issue is that I coveted my independence and never let myself need anyone. I'll have to deal with being totally reliant on you and you'll have to selflessly be there for me."

Both beings turn to the teacher supervising the gathering for her final approval of their arrangement and she nods her assent. Then, the two approach each other and embrace, committing themselves with great love to help each other grow in this next cycle. And all the other souls who witness this applaud with admiration and support.

Now it's your turn to stand and address the group. "I really need your help on this one," you begin. "For many lives now, I have not loved myself very much. I've been in awful emotional situations and never left. I've tolerated all kinds of mistreatment and been so passive that I never even spoke up. I cannot allow this to continue. I've given this serious thought and this time, I am ready to heal this pattern once and for all. But I need something really big to wake me up, because as soon as I'm in a human body, I seem to forget who I really am."

All of the beings murmur their approval at what you have just said. They, too, know what it is like to return to the earth plane and forget why they came back in the first place. And each of them has had moments such as this one, in which desperate measures are called for.

One of the great teachers steps forward. "I have something in mind that would be ideal," she suggests. She calls out the name of a soul sitting near you. Instantly, you recognize this being, someone you have loved many times, someone you trust very much.

"Don't you owe this soul a favor of love?" she asks your friend.

"Yes, great one," your friend answers reverently. "Several lifetimes ago, she played the part of my wife and her love helped me free myself of terrible guilt I'd carried with me for a long time. I owe her an enormous debt."

"Very well," the teacher replies. "She needs to be pushed to finally choose to honor herself. Once again, in this next incarnation, you will play the role of her husband, only this time you will be thoughtless, unfaithful, and relentlessly cruel, until she cannot bear it any longer and loves herself enough to leave you. Then, she will have broken her cycle of many lifetimes and never again will she mistreat herself. *Only because she trusts you so deeply will she allow you to play this role for her.* This is why I have chosen you. Once you do this, your debt will be repaid and you will be able to live out the rest of that life as a good person."

The teacher turns toward you. "Do you accept this arrangement?" she asks.

Your heart leaps with joy as you realize that finally, after so many attempts in so many lives, you will achieve this breakthrough! And your dear friend is going to be the one to help you! You can hardly contain your excitement and gratitude.

"Yes, I accept," you reply. You walk toward your friend, who has agreed out of his great love for you to play such a difficult role in your next life.

"I promise I won't let you down," this being assures you. "I will behave so badly that you will be forced to love yourself enough to leave."

"Thank you, dear one," you say, reaching out to embrace him.

Like this, the cosmic gathering continues, each being agreeing to play the perfect role for the other. Once the main characters on your list have been cast, you fill in the minor ones until you have made hundreds of agreements with hundreds of other souls to be one another's teachers. All of these decisions are made with great love, great compassion, and great courage. Then, you sit back and wait for the perfect moment to be born into the family made up of souls who've already agreed to play the roles of your parents, and like this you begin the next phase of your spiritual journey.

And as soon as you are born, you forget all of this.

Twenty-five years later, you meet a man with whom you instantly fall in love, and in spite of the fact that he has a terrible temper and you suspect he's still sleeping with his former girlfriend, you agree to marry him. Your friends and family think you're crazy and secretly, you can't quite figure out why you put up with him, but it all somehow feels like it's meant to be.

Ten years will pass during which you will be horribly mistreated and in spite of all your efforts to get this man to change, he will continue to be abusive, until one day, you find the strength you haven't had before and you leave, vowing that never again will you be with anyone who doesn't love you the way you deserve to be loved. And as you sit in your tiny apartment that first night, alone, lonely, frightened, crying your eyes out but proud of yourself, knowing you did the right thing, somewhere on the heavenly plane, a wise teacher will be smiling.

Did you read this and conclude that I have a very vivid imagination? Or did something in you say, "Yes, this makes sense. Yes, deep inside of me, I feel the truth in it." How would your life change if this scenario *were* true? How would you approach your relationships differently if you believed that you had, indeed, hand-picked every one of them? How would you feel about the people you encountered if you remembered that each one was a soul who had agreed to play a particular role in your spiritual growth?

It is my conviction that this is, indeed, the way things are—that our souls consent to undergo every experience we have here on earth, including all of our relationships. It's as if some cosmic computer figures out exactly what each of us needs and sends the perfect people our way. Every friend, every enemy, every lover, everyone who breaks our hearts, every family member, every business partner, all of them are in our lives for one reason—*to help us become more loving human beings.* Granted, it may not seem like they are helping us. It may appear that, quite to the contrary, they are hurting us, or holding us back, or making us miserable, or driving us crazy. However, their presence isn't designed to torment us, but to teach us something essential about ourselves that we need to learn.

This is the eighth principle:

SECRET NUMBER EIGHT:

ALL RELATIONSHIPS ARE YOUR MIRRORS AND ALL PEOPLE ARE YOUR TEACHERS

Remember Secret Number Two: *The purpose of your life is for you to grow into the best human being you can be.* This means that life uses everything, each circumstance and encounter, to help you grow. And so the purpose of your relationships is the same—for you to grow into the most loving human being possible. If this is how relationships are designed, then it follows that the people with whom you are actually in relationships are also there to help you to grow—they are your teachers. In some way, they will stretch you to develop new emotional skills, to gain new spiritual insights, to become a more loving being. *And many times they do this by behaving in ways that show you exactly where your weaknesses are.*

> Ultimately, the purpose of relationships
> is to help us become more loving human beings,
> and one way they do this is to show us
> everything about ourselves that isn't loving
> enough yet.

Who Are Your Loved Ones?

Can anyone push your emotional buttons as infuriatingly as your intimate partner? Can anyone lure the worst parts of your personality up to the surface as effectively as your own children? Can anyone make you feel as out of control and volatile as your own family members? Can anyone make you feel as much, put up with as much, or react as much as those with whom you are in intimate relationships? We each know the answers to these questions all too well—*no!*

Relationships are the perfect classroom in which you can learn your most important life lessons and your loved ones are the perfect teachers. Why? **Because the people you love will be able to affect you in ways no one else can. They will be able to get to you more profoundly, probe more deeply, push you up against your issues more effectively.**

Imagine, for a moment, that you wanted to hire a spy to infiltrate a company. Your preference would be someone who already had access to the company's top personnel, someone who was trusted, who would be able to get into places and situations an outsider couldn't. The better known the spy, the more deeply he could penetrate the organization and the more effective he would be.

I believe this same principle applies to why it's the people we love the most that often bring us our greatest challenges and teach us our harshest lessons—*because we will allow them to get to us in ways no one else could.* They can infiltrate our hearts, sneaking past our usual protections, and arriving at the core of our vulnerability, our fear, our longings. Once there, they begin to do the work they've been "hired" (by us!) to do—to help us become aware of any emotional wounds that need to be healed, false beliefs that need to be corrected, unhealthy behavioral habits that need to be changed.

You'll recall that, at the cosmic gathering you read about earlier, one of the wise teachers needed to choose someone who would treat you terribly in order for you to finally get strong and leave. She chose a soul she knew you loved and trusted deeply. Only someone with whom you have this kind of timeless connection could take you through such an intense process of attachment, pain, and revelation.

Have you ever met someone you ended up falling in love with and from the first moment, you felt as if you've known this person forever, as if you were experiencing a reunion and not an introduction? Perhaps that's because you have, indeed, found an ancient companion, a loved one with whom you've traveled many times before. Sometimes these familiar souls come into our lives simply to love and support us, often as dear friends. Other times, they play more dramatic, passionate roles as our lovers, our parents, our children, and frequently, our heart-breakers. But one thing is for sure— they never leave without having changed us, and taught us love's most important lessons.

How Love Teaches Us Our Most Essential Lessons

How do these loved ones teach you? It usually isn't by sitting down and patiently explaining ways in which you need to be a more caring person, or calmly pointing out areas that need improvement. *It's by doing or saying things that make it difficult for you to love them or yourself as much as you should; it's by behaving in ways that challenge your strengths and expose your weaknesses;*

it's by showing you your vulnerabilities and pulling you off center.

Your loved ones act like a mirror:
they force you to look at everything about yourself
that is not loving
and then they stretch you into learning to love more.

Sit down and make a list of every important relationship you've been in, including friendships, business associations, etc. Next to each name, write down what was difficult about that relationship and what you most disliked about interacting with that person. Then, ask yourself what you learned from that experience and how you changed. You will be amazed to discover that, without exception, you were being forced to grow, forced to become more flexible, more compassionate, more steady, more loving toward yourself and others. And your most challenging relationships will probably also have been the most transformational.

When I reach back into my own life, I find so many marvelous examples of this:

- The boyfriend in college who was sweet, but not the smartest guy in the world. In order to have any kind of emotional conversation with him without his blowing up in anger, I had to

be totally clear about what I was saying, pain-
fully methodical, and carefully explain every
nuance of my feelings. *His slow mind forced
me to learn clarity, precision, and patience in
communication.*

• The lover who refused to get involved in
personal growth and thought everything I
was doing was foolish. No matter how hard I
tried, he would not budge on his views, and I
ended up constantly having to defend my
commitment to my spiritual path. *His closed-
mindedness forced me to articulate and deepen
my dedication to inner work, and eventually
choose it although it meant sacrificing a life with
him.*

• The friend who was always getting upset with
me over inconsequential things, making me
continually "earn" her approval. She was
moody, secretive, and had a list of rules people
had to follow in order to please her. Naturally,
I always failed at something and would feel
hurt, rejected, and apologetic, even though I
didn't feel I'd done anything wrong. *Her very
conditional love showed me the part of my personality that was desperate for the approval of
others regardless of how they treated me, the
lengths to which I'd go to be loved, and ulti-*

mately, how good I felt when I ended the relationship and realized I didn't need everyone to like me.

- The employee who was a chronic liar, covering up her mistakes and continually letting me down in my business. Time and time again, my inner voice would warn me that something was wrong and I would ignore it, choosing to believe her nervous and defensive explanations rather than my own intuition. Finally, her ineptitude caused some serious financial problems and I fired her. *Her incompetence and dishonesty taught me how reluctant I was to pay attention to the details of my own business, how easily I allowed myself to be talked out of my own truth, and, as I was forced to rebuild my financial structure, gave me great confidence that I could start over.*

- The mate who constantly put me down, criticized every aspect of my life, and used sex and affection as a punishment or reward for whether or not I was pleasing him. In spite of how unhealthy this relationship was, I stayed far longer than I should have, hoping he would change, hoping I would figure out how to make him happy, lowering my standards for how I deserved to be treated so I didn't have to be alone. *This man's emotional abuse*

> *showed me how little I was willing to accept in*
> *love, how stubborn and prideful I was about try-*
> *ing to make things work even when they obvi-*
> *ously couldn't, how much I hated "giving up"*
> *on anything, and that how people treated me*
> *was ultimately up to me.*

What profound and life-changing lessons these people taught me! Each one showed me important pieces of myself I needed to look at, and, by playing their often objectionable roles perfectly, pushed me into loving myself more and becoming a more conscious human being. Naturally, in addition, we all have dozens of people on our love list who, by treating us wonderfully, have taught us trust, caring, and gratitude. I chose some of the more extreme examples on my own list, however, to illustrate that even those relationships we think were "bad" are perhaps the ones in which we grew the most.

Even brief encounters with people give you the opportunity to develop loving qualities as you respond to them:

Slow people teach you patience.
Angry people teach you evenness and stillness.
Abusive people teach you self-respect.
Emotionally shut-down people teach you
    unconditional love.
Dishonest people teach you integrity.
Stubborn people teach you flexibility.
Frightened people teach you courage.

Secret Number Eight is one of the spiritual principles I try to remember whenever I interact with anyone. Especially when someone does something that upsets me, challenges me, annoys me, or worse, I ask myself:

What has this person been sent to teach me?
What quality am I lacking in this moment that is making me suffer?

So if I'm standing in line at the post office and the clerk is taking forever, and the line hasn't moved for ten minutes, and I catch myself thinking, "She is sooooo dumb. Where do they find these people?" I can stop, take a deep breath, and ask, "What has this person been sent to teach me?" *Patience. Tolerance.* Or if I'm sitting in a business meeting and a colleague loses his temper, I can ask myself, "What has this raving maniac been sent to teach me?" *Evenness. Stillness.* I don't have to react. I can remain centered.

Why Do These People Keep Finding Me?

This past summer, I shared this concept about the mirror of relationships with a dear friend of mine. Several days later, as we were having lunch, she told me about some strange experiences she was having.

"Barbara, I've noticed recently that creepy people seem to be attracted to me and it's driving me crazy."

"What do you mean, creepy people?" I asked.

"Weird people, like this strange woman I hardly know at work who keeps telling me odd details about her personal life as if we were close friends, and this woman I met once at a party who keeps calling me, saying she is sure we are meant to be close because we are psychic twins. And this man who asked me out once, and who I said no to, who keeps leaving messages on my answering machine, describing his day and what he watched on TV last night. It's totally creepy!"

"I agree," I nodded. "It does sound creepy. What do you make of it?"

"I can't figure it out," she said, shaking her head. "I keep thinking about what you said about everyone being my teacher, but these people are just nuts!"

"Well, keep contemplating it," I suggested. "I'm sure it's all happening for some reason—it's too strange to be accidental."

Two nights later, my friend called me, very excited. "I figured it out!" she announced. "It's about my boundaries, or my lack of them. I've never been good at setting boundaries, with my ex-husband, my kids, even people at work. I am too concerned about everyone liking me, I guess. So there is this part of me that is nice to people I don't want to be nice to and that says *yes* when I want to say *no*, and doesn't want to hurt anyone's feelings. I think these people I mentioned must have somehow picked this up and concluded that it's O.K. to invade my space like they do. It's really showing me how angry I feel when I let people in past where I want them to be, and how I need to set clearer boundaries with everyone."

I was so proud of my friend for arriving at this profound conclusion. She was right—it was as if the cosmic computer assigned these pushy people to bug her, scheduling one after the other, until she finally got fed up and examined the issue she'd been avoiding for a long time. It would have been so easy for her to just decide these people were crazy and leave it at that. But she used this principle to look more closely at what was really happening and learned a valuable lesson.

Relationships, even casual ones, have a much higher agenda than we could ever imagine. They are each gifts in disguise. A hundred times a day, you are offered the opportunity to grow. Be on the lookout for your teachers. You never know in what unusual or mysterious form they'll appear.

The Mirror of Relationships

Recently, someone sent me this little love story:

Once upon a time, there was an earthworm crawling through the grass on a beautiful summer day. He was lonely, and as he slithered along the ground, he thought to himself, "If only I could find a soul mate, I would be happy!"

Suddenly, he looked up, and there before him was another earthworm, brown and slinky and beautiful. In an instant, he fell madly in love.

"My darling," he crooned, "at last I have found you! Come away with me forever!"

And the object he was looking at said, "Be quiet, you silly fool! I am just your other end . . ."

Perhaps our loved ones aren't virtually connected to us like the other end of that earthworm, but in many ways it is, indeed, our own reflection we react to in our intimate relationships. After all, we fall in love with people we either feel are already like us, or whom we wish we were more like. We gravitate toward qualities we admire, characteristics that are familiar. "We're so much alike!" we announce triumphantly, certain that we have made the correct choice. On the other hand, the more dissimilar someone is from us, the more we usually want nothing to do with him or her. And we often work hard to erase any differences we do discover, in the name of becoming more compatible. Ironically, however, it is these very differences which can teach us the most about ourselves.

Relationships will often make you uncomfortable
as they force you to look into the mirror at yourself.
The qualities you dislike in others
often reflect parts of who you are
with which you haven't yet come to terms.

If you measure the success of your relationship in terms of how comfortable it makes you feel, you may make the mistake of concluding that your relationship is unhealthy because, from time to time, it's pushing all of your buttons. Guess what? *It's supposed to push your buttons! Your partner is supposed to have some qualities that challenge you. That's his job!* If you have issues about needing everything to be perfect, he will probably be a slob. If you have a difficult time expressing your emotions, he will probably always probe to find out how you're feeling. If you are impatient, he will probably be an incurable procrastinator.

Many years ago, I was briefly involved with someone who'd had what I considered an easy life. He came from a very wealthy family and all of his business opportunities manifested through connections. He seemed to know the right people and always be in the right place at the right time. Almost overnight, he became extremely successful. Consequently, he didn't work very hard, and in fact, was quite lazy.

In the beginning of our relationship, I admired this man very much and was impressed with how cool and calm he was about his career. But within a few months, I began feeling extremely resentful of what I considered to be his smug attitude, and his laziness began to really turn me off. I would be in the study working and hear him watching television in the living room and become really upset. "How can he just lie around like that?" I'd fume. "It makes me sick."

Whenever I'd make a thinly veiled critical comment about how much time he spent doing nothing, he'd respond, "I don't have to work hard—my money is working for me." And I'd only become more furious at him, concluding that I just couldn't respect his values. Needless to say, we broke up.

Now, I look back on this relationship and see it so differently. *This man was a mirror for me, reflecting back a part of myself I refused to accept*—that piece of me that wished I, too, could lie around and do nothing, that wanted someone to take care of me, that wished I didn't have to always work so hard to accomplish everything. I'd always prided myself on my ability to set goals and achieve them, to work harder than anyone else. But hidden beneath my dogmatic work ethic was a wild, carefree woman who just wanted to have fun! I didn't trust her and had a lot of judgments about her character, so I kept that part of me locked deep inside.

This man appeared in my life to embody the very qualities I condemned. No wonder he made me so angry—that's how I felt about that lazy, self-indulgent part of myself! *I was angry at my own reflection.* And even though I know we weren't meant to have a long-term relationship, I wish I'd realized that he was just a mirror. Then, I could have ended our love affair without making him so wrong for being the way he was and perhaps even admitting that I wished I could be more easygoing like him.

Take a moment and think about all the qualities in your loved ones that you find obnoxious, distasteful, awful, and generally unlovable. Consider that they may embody the very qualities in yourself that you find unacceptable, parts of your personality that you have rejected or suppressed, and parts of your being that you do not love. And the stronger your reaction, the more likely it is that this characteristic is one you have really been hiding from.

> Whether your relationship lasts for
> six minutes, six months, or sixty years,
> remember that this person is in your life
> to teach you something,
> and that much of what you *think* you see in him
> will really be your own reflection in the mirror
> of his heart.

When you find yourself reacting intensely to something in another person, ask yourself:

> How can I use this reaction to learn something
>   about myself?
> What part of me is like this person?
> What is this situation trying to teach me?

Remembering Your Highest Purpose in Love

It's not always easy, in the midst of an argument with your lover, when you are sure he is behaving badly, to look at him and think, "Oh, my wonderful teacher! How I adore you!" And it's difficult, when the person you love seems to be causing you great pain and heartache, to believe that some higher part of you actually wants this to be happening so you will learn a lesson. *Yet this is the path of conscious love—for you and your partner to remember your highest purpose in coming together.*

Here are three truths about the path of conscious love:

1. **We have been brought together for the purpose of helping each other grow and we will be each other's teacher.**

2. **Our relationship is a precious gift. It will take us through whatever we need to learn to become more conscious, loving human beings.**

3. **The challenges and difficulties we experience will always illuminate our most needed lessons.**

When you make a commitment to accept this purposeful vision of love, you begin to experience the struggles and problems you encounter in a sacred context. When you argue, when you are angry at each other, when you get frustrated and feel like turning away, this vision shines like a beacon of light in the fog, reminding you that there is a higher purpose to the everyday difficulties you're challenged by. *You remember that you have chosen to travel together for a reason and by remembering, you can more quickly move beyond the usual emotional reactions of anger and hurt and look for the lessons that are always present underneath, waiting for you to discover them.*

When the Lesson Is Learned, the Teacher Disappears

Imagine that you hired someone to build a set of shelves in your closet. When the carpenter had completed the job, you would pay him, thank him for a job well done, and say good-bye. Now imagine that, as we saw in our cosmic journey at the beginning of this chapter, your soul had procured the services of another soul to do some work for you in this lifetime and that the work had been completed. What would you do?

What many of us do at these moments is become confused. Even when all signs indicate that the relationship should be over, even when it feels like everything has changed, still, we often cling to the person and refuse to let go. It would be as if you held onto the carpenter as he tried to walk out the door, screaming, "Please don't leave me. There must be some more work you can do here!"

There are people who are meant to be in our lives over a long period of time, teaching us a series of lessons about love. However, there are others who are meant to find us on our path, do what they agreed to do, and then disappear. Sometimes you are the one who realizes your emotional contract with a partner has expired and that you must move on. Sometimes, it is the other person who becomes aware of this first, and only later do you realize that he was right to leave. One thing is for sure—when your lessons with each other have been learned, you will find yourselves being pulled apart in one way or another.

**One of the greatest love lessons we can learn
is knowing when the time has come
for one of our "love teachers" to depart,
and knowing how to let go of him or her
with compassion, forgiveness, and gratitude.**

The great spiritual teacher and writer Ram Dass says that in order to be truly loving, we must rerun everything through our "compassion machine." We must look beyond what people *appear* to be or have been to us, and remember who they really are: expressions of pure spirit, fellow travelers who have come into our lives dressed up as our lovers or children or parents or enemies, but who, in the end, are only there to serve one purpose—to teach us about love.

In his classic book *Be Here Now*, Ram Dass writes: *"You must see that all beings are just beings . . . and that all the wrappings of personality and role and body are the coverings. Your attachments are only to the coverings, and as long as you are attached to someone else's covering you are stuck, and you keep them stuck, in that attachment. Only when you can see the essence, can see God, in each human being do you free yourself and those about you. It's hard work when you have spent years building a fixed model of who someone else is to abandon it, but until that model is superseded by a compassionate model, you are still stuck."*

• • •

There is a classic Buddhist story about a man who was traveling for many years on a pilgrimage to holy places. At one point he began walking along the side of a wide river. Now, the side on which he walked was very rocky and dangerous, thus slowing his progress and making his days strenuous. When he looked across the river, he noticed that the other side was flat and smooth, appearing to be much easier to walk on.

"I want to go to that side of the river," he decided, "but I have no way of getting across. What should I do?"

So the aspirant sat down to meditate and received a message to build a raft out of branches and mud. And this is what he did. He spent days constructing a raft, drying it in the sun until finally it was ready. Then, he laid the raft in the water, stepped onto it, and safely crossed to the other side.

As he pulled the raft out of the river, the man thought to himself, "You know, this raft has been so useful to me, and I worked so hard to build it. I cannot just abandon it here on the riverbank. The wood will rot and the rain will wash it away until it disintegrates. No, I cannot do this to the raft—I will carry it with me."

So that is what the man did. He pulled the heavy raft onto his back and began to walk, dragging it behind him as he struggled to take his now even more difficult steps. And this is how he traveled.

The teaching in this story is that even a good thing that has been useful to us becomes an unnecessary burden when we no longer need it. *That which we no longer need should be set aside, or it weighs us down.* And when we leave behind what doesn't serve us anymore, we must do so not with condemnation, but with gratitude.

From Heartbreaking to Healing

Remember the man I wrote about in the previous chapter? Did you read that story and think, "What a jerk! How could he have deceived Barbara like that?" Perhaps you would be surprised to know that I consider him one of the great teachers of my life. *Nothing but the horribly painful experiences he put me through could have possibly forced me to look at myself as deeply as I did afterward.* No normal breakup could have achieved so much. I needed every last detail of that soap opera to dig out my projections, my illusions, my emotional habits that had always gotten me into trouble.

In the many months of healing that followed the end of that relationship, I came to realize how perfectly this man had set me up for rejection and, ultimately, for revelation. He pulled every one of my issues out of me, then vanished, and I was left staring at my own stuff—how I gave away too much of myself even when I wasn't getting an equal amount back; how I paid more attention to what I could offer someone rather than to what, if anything, he was offering me; how I went too far, too fast, longing to unite, even when the other person wasn't ready. I had examined these unhealthy tendencies many times, but never before had they been so apparent, or so dramatically presented. And it was the very intensity of the situation that acted as an enormous wake-up call.

From the point of view of making me feel good in the moment, this man had failed miserably. But from the point of view of teaching me about myself, he had succeeded in ways no one else ever had. So was he an enemy or a great friend to my soul? Was his presence in my life a curse or a profound blessing to my path of growth? These were my contemplations as I worked to understand the events that had occurred during that painful period of time.

My conclusion: *This person was an ancient friend who had taken on the task of teaching me one of the most painful yet important lessons of this lifetime.* Our timeless connection drew me to him the instant I met him and he did the job he was supposed to do. He was, indeed, a blessing, not a curse, and his presence in my life was a remarkable turning point in my spiritual development.

When we remember that our loved ones are our teachers,
our attitude toward them can shift
from resentment and blame to love and gratitude.

So here is the surprising end of my story with that man who broke my heart: *I wrote him a thank-you letter!* Although I didn't express my gratitude for *what* he'd done or condone his behavior, I thanked him for what I had gained from the whole process. I shared everything with him that I've shared with you and told him that I believed we had agreed to go through this dramatic experience together. "I must have loved you and trusted you deeply from long ago," I wrote, "to allow you to teach me such a profound lesson. And you must have really loved me to agree to play such an unappealing role in my life, all for the purpose of freeing me to love in a way I never have before."

I am sure that consciously, this man didn't understand most of what I said, but I am also sure that his higher self did hear me. Some time later he called, and apologized for all the ways in which he'd hurt me, and today we are friends. In reaching out to him, I gave myself a great gift—*the gift of forgiveness*—for me, for him, for what we agreed to undergo, for the harsh ways love sometimes teaches us what we need to learn.

Imagine it is the end of your life. Your consciousness leaves this body and you feel light, free, and at peace. Effortlessly, you find yourself traveling through many dimensions of reality, until you arrive back at that place of light that only now, once again, you remember having come from. You feel overjoyed to be here, to have completed this latest adventure on your journey, to be home.

One of the great, ancient teachers welcomes you, inviting you to enter a beautiful space filled with a warm, glowing light. And now you remember—it is time for your ceremony of completion, something in which all souls must participate when they arrive back from the other world. The wise being nods her agreement: "Yes, dear one," she says, "all of the souls who played the roles of your teachers are gathered here to greet you, so you can honor them for how they served you and express your gratitude."

You look up and there before you, you see them, each who was an important part of your recent time on earth, each smiling at you with so much love, free now from any need to pretend they are anything other than your dearest spiritual companions. One by one, you will walk up to the souls before you, standing in front of them in the formal manner required in a completion ceremony, your hands folded in front of your heart, and you will speak to them.

You watch someone else who is just finishing their ceremony. She approaches a soul who played the role of her husband. "Thank you, dear one," she begins, "for teaching me about love. From you, I learned to give even when it did not seem I was getting back what I thought I needed. This was a great lesson which I cherish. *I honor you for being my teacher.*" The two souls embrace.

Next, she approaches a soul who played the role of her father. "Thank you, dear one," she says, "for teaching me about love. From you, I learned to respect my own values and opinions, even when you diminished them. I know this was a painful part for you to play with me, and it taught me a great lesson which I had been waiting to learn for a long time. *I honor you for being my teacher.*" And she embraces this soul with great joy.

• • •

N ow, it is your turn.

Who would be standing there in front of you?
Who would you thank for teaching you about love?
Who would you honor for teaching you the lessons
   you needed to learn?
What would you say to each one?
And, when it was their turn, who would thank you?

True Freedom Comes from How You Respond to Life and Not from What Life Does to You

*Our lives are a sum total
of the choices we have made.*

DR. WAYNE W. DYER

What do you think it would take for you to feel really free? Would you need to have a lot of money in the bank? Would you need to know you were going to meet the perfect person and live happily ever after? Would you need to be forewarned about everything that would be taking place in your future, so you were prepared and in control?

I know someone who has this kind of freedom, but not because of her riches, or her perfect mate, or a magical guarantee that everything in her life will turn out fine. No, this person possesses a gift more valuable than the most precious treasure: *She is the master of her own destiny.*

Who is this fortunate woman? *She is you!*

Whether you know it or not, you already have all the freedom you could ever desire. And you have it right now, in this very moment.

This moment is always all you have.

Right now, you are not yet in tomorrow and you are no longer in yesterday. You are here now, and you are free to do with this moment what you want. You can make it a painful moment. You can make it a grateful moment. You can make it a frightened moment. You can make it a courageous moment. *How this moment turns out is up to you, and only you.*

"But that's not true," you may be thinking. "What if my boyfriend calls me and says he doesn't love me anymore? What if my kids start acting up and make me late for work? What if my car breaks down and I can't get to my important meeting? These things aren't up to me."

You're right. The events that occur in your life aren't always up to you. You can't control other people or outside circumstances. But you *can* control how you react to them. How you respond to these people and events *is* up to you.

You may not be able to control what happens *to* you, but you can control what happens *within* you.

This is such an important distinction to remember and it is what each and every secret in this book is about. These timeless principles remind you that *living from the inside out* is the only way you can really take control of your life. Your true freedom isn't found in your ability to do anything you want, or go anywhere you dream of, or have anything you long for. It is the freedom you have to create your own reality by how you respond to life in this and every moment.

Here is the ninth principle:

SECRET NUMBER NINE:

**TRUE FREEDOM COMES FROM
HOW YOU RESPOND TO LIFE
AND NOT FROM WHAT LIFE
DOES TO YOU**

True freedom has nothing to do with anything on the outside. It has to do with your ability to find the gift in each and every moment, to use each experience to learn, and to maintain your center regardless of what is happening to you.

> You can learn to be happy *in* a situation
> even if you can't be happy *with* a situation.

We began considering this principle in our first secret: *Everything you need to be happy is inside of you.* If you base your happiness on the outer events of your life, you are giving your power away to other people and to circumstances beyond your control. Secret Number Nine reminds you that *your power lies in your choice:*

> *You choose how to respond to what life puts in*
>   *front of you.*
> *You choose how to understand it.*
> *You choose how to feel about it.*
> *You choose what to do with it.*

Choosing to Respond and Not to React

Did you know that dozens of times a day, you are involved in a very spiritual practice? It is a practice that determines whether you will create a state of turmoil or contentment in your consciousness that either fills you with panic or peace. This spiritual practice happens without your even realizing it and yet it is one of the most important things you do. What am I referring to?

> It is your choice to either *react* or *respond*
> to the challenging situations with which
> you are confronted.

Understanding the difference between these two words is the secret for creating true freedom for yourself from moment to moment. Think about the word *react*. It's actually has two parts: *re* and *act*. To react, to act again, to repeat an action. Most of the time in our lives, this is what we do—we re-act. When we are faced with a difficult situation, we unconsciously choose to act as we always have, *to react habitually*. Someone forgets to do something for you and you suddenly find yourself getting annoyed. Your husband is a little distant and your mind instantly concludes something must be wrong. You make an error at work and right away, you start criticizing yourself.

These habitual reactions are the result of a lifetime of emotional programming. They're the first choice you usually make, especially when you're under pressure, frightened, or feeling stressed. The problem is that many of these reactions are unhealthy, and don't serve your highest good. They come from fear, from pride, from confusion. Of course, you're not even aware that you're reacting in these ways—that's why they're called "reactions."

Now let's look at *respond*: It has the same root as the word *responsibility*, the word *spondère*, from the Old French, which means "to pledge." To respond means *to act with responsibility*, with awareness, to repledge yourself to your highest purpose, and therefore, to be conscious about how you react, *and to understand that how you react will be responsible for your state of mind.*

When you *react* without being conscious of what you're doing, you are practicing being unconscious. When you *respond* by being aware of what you are doing, you are practicing being conscious. This is why I said you are engaging in spiritual practices many times a day!

The essence of Secret Number Nine is to make responding consciously (as opposed to reacting unconsciously) the way you move through your life.

When you learn how to stop habitually reacting in life and start consciously responding to life, then you become truly independent, truly powerful, truly free.

Find Your Center and Act from There

How can you learn to stop reacting and start responding? It sounds inspiring, but when you discover your three-year-old with paint all over his hair, or when your mate tells you that he doesn't want to talk about what's bothering him, or when one of your best clients switches to another company, you may have a difficult time remembering to respond, and instead, find yourself having some pretty strong reactions! So how can you begin to practice this secret?

By now you know I like taking you on imaginary journeys to stretch your mind, and it's time for another one.

So, imagine that you have traveled back in history, to a period hundreds of years ago. You are a warrior princess and the head of a vast army fighting to protect your lands. You are standing in the middle of an enormous battlefield and all around you is chaos. Everywhere, there are soldiers in fierce combat with swords and clubs, some on horseback, some on foot. There is the sound of armor and spears clashing and the sound of death. You know you must make immediate and crucial decisions about what course of action to take, but in the midst of so much confusion, it's hard to even think clearly let alone see a solution. You feel the panic rising inside you and know that reacting from this state of fear will only result in a loss of everything you hold dear. What are you going to do?

Then, you get an idea. You ride your horse swiftly

out of the battlefield, away from the madness, and up to the top of a high hill overlooking the scene. There, at the peak, you stop and from your vantage point, you look back at the situation you just left behind. At first, it still looks like utter chaos, but soon you begin to see things you could not when you were in the midst of the fray. You notice weak spots in your opponents' forces; you become aware of what areas need more reinforcements; and you can even see a possibility for taking your enemies by surprise that wasn't apparent before.

Confident that you can now respond with clarity, you ride back down the hill, ready to give your orders.

Welcome back from your stint as a warrior princess. Although most of us are living in safer, less violent times, in some ways every day of our lives is still like that battlefield. Yes, our enemies are not as deadly—they may simply be projects we need to get done, or our misbehaving children, or our moody mate, or the pressures of being a single parent, or any of the thousands of things that can and do go wrong every day that make our lives seem to be a war zone. And like the ancient warrior, we may often look around at all that is causing us anxiety and stress and feel totally overwhelmed. We're not sure how to handle a situation; we don't know if we should say something to this person who's upsetting us or not; we don't know if we're overreacting to a problem or if we really should be concerned. We don't know if it's time to make a change or to wait. We just can't see clearly.

How did our warrior solve her problem? *She rode away from it.* And this is our solution, as well—*to go in what seems to be the opposite direction from where we need to go.* Instead of habitually responding, we need to pull away from the actions of our life, from the movement, and find our center, the still point, the inner point that is not moving and not changing. From there, we will be able to see the truth. From there, we will be able to respond.

This technique of learning how to respond can be summed up in the phrase:

"Find your center and act from there."

Where is that center, the equivalent of that quiet hilltop? We all have this place inside ourselves—we talked about it in our chapter on the mind. Some people call it the witness, some call it the inner spirit, some call it the true self. No matter how you name that center within you, its characteristics are the same: It is that which is nonchanging in you, that which always stays the same no matter what is happening on the outside. It is your source of wisdom, of peace, of love.

Most of the time, our attention is so focused on our outer world that we may not even be aware of this center of peace and power within ourselves. But it *is* there, and it never goes away. We never lose it. The truth is:

That source of love and peace never moves away
from you—
you move away from it.

What moves us off of our center? How do we get so disconnected from ourselves? For one thing, we don't take the time to visit that place, to become familiar with it, to use it as a refuge as well as a great resource. We get so busy trying to manipulate the outside, as we have already seen, that we forget to connect to the inside. And the more we're caught up in our outer life, the more difficult it may be to find our way back inside again.

Finding your true freedom means finding a way to connect back to your center and making this reconnection with yourself a regular part of your life. Once you arrive at that place in the center, you will be able to look out at the circle of your life that surrounds you with all its facets, and see things much more clearly.

There's a Buddhist saying:

> *"When the lake is churned up, nothing can be seen.*
> *When the lake is still, all can be seen."*

Finding your center means regularly taking time to still the lake of your mind, to allow the waves of reactivity to settle down. Beneath those waves is a wondrous and peaceful place. It is beyond your reactions, beyond your thoughts. It is the place all thoughts come from, the source of pure intelligence, pure awareness.

This still place within you is the source of your true wisdom, your true voice. When you can be quiet enough to hear that inner voice, it will guide you in the right direction on your journey; it will reveal the path you need to take at each crossroads you come to; it will show you how to respond to whatever you encounter along the way. That's because when you enter that place of inner stillness, you are inviting God's voice to fill you.

The great spiritual teacher Meister Eckehart said, "The very best and utmost of attainment in this life is to remain still and let God act and speak in thee."

How the Habit of Stillness May Have Saved My Life

Recently I had a very dramatic experience that reminded me of the immeasurable benefits I receive from the practice of finding my center. I was driving back from Palm Springs to Los Angeles on a very uncharacteristically stormy afternoon in Southern California. Everyone goes very fast on this particular stretch of freeway in the desert, and I was moving along with the rest of the traffic, which included many big rig trucks. The rain was coming down so heavily at times that it was difficult to see and it took all of my concentration to keep my car steady on the road.

Suddenly, I heard a loud sound like an explosion and my car began to career wildly out of control. One of my tires had blown totally off and the vehicle was thrown off balance, skidding dangerously out of the left lane I was in and heading on a zigzag course toward the guard rail at seventy miles an hour. I had no idea what to do, whether I should brake or not, turn the wheel in one direction or another, and for a second I just froze and thought, "This is how I am going to die."

Then, the strangest thing happened. For a moment, it was as if everything stopped, suspended in time, like someone had pushed the pause button on the VCR. Then, movement started again, but in very slow motion. I felt like I was watching myself in a movie, only I wasn't in control. I could feel the car still sliding all over the highway; I could hear the huge trucks whizzing by and feel the water they sprayed as they passed so I couldn't see a thing. I could feel my heart pounding in my chest. But I felt very quiet, very still, as if I was in deep meditation. And in that state, I noticed that some force seemed to have taken over my hands and was steering the car in a particular manner. I was sure that someone else's hands were actually gripping the wheel and could sense a powerful presence in control. It was as if I had disappeared.

In what seemed to be minutes later, but was probably only seconds, I found myself sitting on the shoulder of the freeway, the car stopped and just safely out of the way of traffic by a few feet. I was amazed to notice that I felt totally calm, my inner state undisturbed by the outer events. I had no idea how I'd gotten the car in control and out of danger or how I'd avoided crashing into the railing. I hadn't made any conscious decision to steer a certain way or use the brakes in a particular manner, since I didn't know much about these things. Yet something had taken charge and whatever it was had most probably saved my life.

I called the emergency roadside service, and as I waited for the tow truck to arrive, I contemplated what had just happened. Where had I gone for those twenty or thirty seconds? Why wasn't I panicking? Why had everything seemed so quiet? Slowly, it began to dawn on me. For thirty years, I had been formally practicing meditation almost every day and my consciousness was in the habit of becoming very quiet, very calm. *In that moment of crisis, my awareness had taken refuge in its familiar state of inner stillness.* I had, in essence, gone into meditation, and from that place of pure intelligence, some power higher than my conscious mind had taken over and known exactly what to do. Without even deciding to, I had found my center and acted from there.

When the tow truck driver was giving me a lift back to his service station, my car hooked up behind him, he shared something that was even more astonishing. "You know, you had nothing left but metal where that tire used to be," he explained. "I have to tell you, that in this rain and going as fast as you were just on that metal rim, it's a miracle that you didn't crash into the railing or the traffic. You must have a guardian angel or something watching over you, miss."

"You're right," I replied softly. "I'm sure I do."

I came very close to dying that afternoon. And I am certain that if it weren't for my habit of finding my center through meditation, I would have panicked and not known what to do to save myself. Because I totally got my mind out of the way, that guardian angel did have room to take the wheel and steer me to safety.

Each of us has what might be called a "home base" for our consciousness, a state of awareness we spontaneously settle into. For some people this home base is fear; for some it's an overactive mind that cannot stop obsessing on everything; for others it's a state of dullness and unconsciousness. The more you cultivate the habit of finding your center in a formal way such as meditation, the easier it will be for that to be your home base and for you to begin living in that serene state all the time.

Acting from the Inside Out

This principle of pulling the awareness back in order to then come out and be more effective in life is actually something we see illustrated in the world around us all the time. If you're teaching a child how to throw a ball, what do you do? You show her that first, she has to reach her arm as far back as she can, and then, when she releases the ball, it will fly through the air with ease and distance. *She must first take the ball in the* opposite *direction of where she wants it to end up.* She pulls back in order to go forward.

Many years ago, my first meditation teacher explained this principle, using the analogy of an archer. In order to make the arrow successfully hit the target, he would say, you must first pull it back on the bow until it is perfectly still and unmoving. Then, you release it and it will go where you want it to go. And it is the same with our awareness. In order to think and act and respond effectively, he would continue, you must first pull your awareness back to a place of stillness and nonmovement. Then, when you come out into activity, you will be clear and powerful.

The ancient Indian scripture the *Bhagavad Gita* teaches this concept about true skill in action and has been used as a primer for understanding the principle of living from the inside out for over a thousand years. "Established in being," it says, "perform action." Establish yourself in that state of inner stillness, and then come out and live your life, knowing you will not be simply reacting, but responding from a source of contentment and peace. Find your center and act from there.

> The more deeply you are able to go within,
> the more powerful and effective you will be
> when you come out.

Whenever people ask me how I have been able to accomplish so much in my life and be so creative, or where I received the ideas for my many books or TV shows, I always give them the same answer: *meditation.* I usually get a lot of raised eyebrows and surprised looks at this response, but I go on to explain this principle of acting from the inside out. The more I have learned to tap into my own source of consciousness, the more powerfully I always emerge, feeling as if I am being carried forward by a wise and benevolent force and lovingly guided in the right direction.

So how can you begin to find your center and respond from the inside out? *The most important commitment you can make is to include some form of inner connection as a regular part of your life.* You can do this through daily meditation, through prayer, or just by taking some time to sit quietly with your eyes closed, becoming aware of the silence between your thoughts. Even a few minutes a day will make a noticeable difference in the quality of your consciousness.

You can also remember this principle as you go about your day. Finding your center means pausing before you say something important to someone. It means taking a moment to pull your awareness inside before you make a crucial business presentation, coming back to center before reacting impulsively in a particular situation, stopping to contemplate before you make a decision based purely on your emotions.

The first step for you might be to just repeat this phrase to yourself whenever you are feeling overwhelmed, frightened, or confused: *Find your center and act from there.* Use it as a mantra. Stop, take some deep breaths, imagine your vision pulling way back or way up, and watch what is going on like you'd watch a movie. Choose to move into that witness consciousness we've talked about. Just this simple act of remembering to think about finding your center will make an instant difference in how you feel.

Have you ever watched a wheel turn? The outermost part of the wheel, the perimeter, goes very fast but the center of the wheel does not move at all. It remains steady, a point of stillness around which all movement can happen. This is a wonderful model for us to remember and aspire to in our own lives—stability in the midst of movement. We learn to become the center of the wheel of our consciousness.

Real stability does not come
from avoiding change and movement,
but knowing that,
because you are anchored to what is nonchanging
within you,
you can ride the waves of outer change
and you can survive their ups and downs.

Using the Secrets About Life Every Day

I've shared many stories with you about how over the years I've used the principles in this book in my own life to create a sense of emotional and spiritual self-reliance. But giving these secrets a name, and writing in such detail about each of them has made me even more conscious of their truth and their power to transform my life, moment by moment. In the course of working on this book, I've created a new practice for myself: *Whenever I am feeling off center, anxious, unhappy, or uncomfortable in any way, I go through the list of ten principles and ask myself which one I am not following in that moment.* Sure enough, I always discover that I am violating one of these basic laws of life and thus causing myself misery. Then, I remind myself of all the advice I gave you and apply it to my own situation immediately. As the saying goes, always teach what we need to learn.

For instance, let's say I have a conversation with a friend that didn't go very well and I get off the phone feeling tense. As soon as I notice that I'm in a state of anxiety, I ask myself:

> **"What truth am I forgetting right now?**
> **What do I need to remember to move**
> **through this?"**

Then, I go through the ten principles in my mind and see how one or many may apply to my present challenge. I stop first at Secret Number Two: *The purpose of life is for you to grow into the best human being you can be.* I remind myself that this experience with my friend is happening for a reason, not because God is persecuting me. And I begin to calm down. Then I move on and remember Secret Number Four: *All obstacles are lessons in disguise—embrace them and learn from them.* I recall the questions I suggested you ask yourself when confronted with difficulties and run through them for myself. "What am I supposed to be learning from this?" etc. I begin to understand more about the conversation with my friend and why I was so sensitive to things he said. Secret Number Five: *Your mind creates your experience of reality, so learn to make your mind your friend.* Instantly I realize that I definitely haven't been doing that. Instead, I've been letting my mind talk me into all kinds of negative scenarios that don't exist, and as soon as I see this, I begin to change my thoughts to positive, loving ones, as we discussed in that chapter. Secret Number Eight: *All relationships are your mirror and all people are your teachers.* I recall that story about choosing our teachers in the life before this world and ask myself, "What did I choose this person to teach me?" This question helps me think about the big picture that is happening between us. And Secret Number Nine: *True freedom comes from how you respond to life and not from what life does to you.* "Yuck," I think to myself. "I have been reacting to that phone call, getting all worked up. No wonder I feel terrible. I need to find my center and act from there." I close my eyes, take some deep breaths, and allow my awareness to travel within. Instantly I feel more calm, more still, and in that quiet space, I see even more about my conversation that I hadn't seen before. Now I know I need to call this person back and express something that will resolve all of the tension between us.

This whole process only takes me a few minutes. By remembering the ten principles, I am able to pull into my highest self, my most wise self, and to take charge of my state of consciousness in the moment. Over the past few months as I've finalized this book, I've practiced this technique of checking in with the ten secrets dozens of times each day. Sometimes I do it enthusiastically; at other times, I have to force myself to read over the list and even at first, my mind sarcastically says: "Yeah, yeah, I know, Number Seven, you're not loving yourself." Bad habits die hard! But eventually, whether it takes me a few minutes or a few hours, I feel myself making a shift from feeling out of control to feeling empowered, from hopelessness to confidence, from anxiety to peace.

I hope you, too, will use these ten principles whenever you are not feeling as good as you want to feel. They are sacred paths you can follow that will easily lead you from your outer world to your inner world, and from fear to freedom in any given moment. Knowing how to retreat to your inner sanctuary and how to call upon your own inner wisdom will give you a sense of faith and security that you could never get from anything on the outside. You go in not to escape, but so that you can reemerge with more strength, more passion, and more courage to create the life you have always wanted.

The supreme Self, the still center of your own being,
holds you together when everything else is falling apart.
Good and bad swirl around like children swinging around
a maypole, but the center holds fast.
Unmoving and untouched,
the supreme Self is totally unaffected by your
ups and downs.
It is eternally blissful and absolutely pure.
GURUMAYI CHIDVILASANANDA

On a recent trip to Florida, I was driving down a two-lane highway that winds through the Florida Keys. The traffic in the lane going in my direction was moving slowly and I noted my increasing discomfort as my car crawled along at twenty miles an hour. I was impatient to get to my destination and had no idea if this was a temporary problem, or if my entire journey would be this frustrating. "I wish I knew what was going on," I thought. Perhaps there was a truck or trailer ahead holding everything up, perhaps there had been an accident, or maybe there was construction on the road.

Suddenly, I saw a large sign on the side of the highway that read:

DON'T WORRY! BE PATIENT!
YOU WILL GET TO A PASSING ZONE IN THREE MILES

I stared at this sign in amazement. It was as if it had been placed in that exact spot just for me, reassuring me that relief was in sight and reminding me to be patient on my journey. I felt so grateful to the employee of the highway department who had decided to use such compassionate and personal language on an official announcement and I relaxed, understanding now that this was obviously a congested area of travel and that soon things would ease up.

I continued driving and noticed that my attitude had completely changed. I was enjoying the beautiful view of the water on either side of the car; I was appreciating the warm breeze that blew in through my windows. I smiled, realizing it was the sign that had changed everything. "Wouldn't it be great if life worked like this?" I remarked to myself. "If every time we were worried or frightened, some cosmic force would come along and say, 'Don't worry! Be patient! You're almost there!'?"

Just as I pondered this fanciful idea of a life in which every occurrence is marked in advance, I saw that I was approaching another sign. When I read the words on it, I burst out laughing: LAKE SURPRISE.

How perfect! Here I was wishing I could have my life mapped out for me, and just at that moment I was coming to Lake Surprise. I shook my head, remembering how many times in my life I'd been traveling toward my own version of Lake Surprise without knowing it. "I sure could have used a warning then," I chuckled to myself as I recalled events I never could have predicted, challenges I never could have imagined would turn up. *And yet I knew that my growth as a soul had occurred from the ways I'd responded to all the Lake Surprises in my life*. Each time I find my way back to my own center, I gain a new sense of strength and freedom that nothing and no one can take away from me.

The roads we travel in our lives may not always be clearly marked or contain such obvious signs of encouragement as that highway in Florida had. But we can be assured that if we are patient, the moment to pass our obstacles and go forward will come and that Lake Surprise will always be just around the bend!

You are the master of your destiny
in each and every moment.

Choose to travel with joy, with passion,
and with complete confidence
that you are always right where you're supposed
to be as long as you are standing
in the still center of your own being.

Whatever the Question, Love Is the Answer

How can you ever hope to know the Beloved
Without becoming in every cell the Lover?
And when you are the Lover at last,
you don't care.
Whatever you know, or don't—only Love is real.

RUMI

This book, like all that is born, was conceived with love. From a place deep inside me, a voice gently but firmly whispered that the time had come for me to share what I'd learned on my own spiritual journey and that in offering this, I would enter a new and exciting phase of my work as a teacher. Like many expectant "mothers," I was both elated and terrified—elated to have the privilege of giving life to something and terrified that I somehow wouldn't do it right, that what came through me wouldn't be as perfect as I hoped it would be.

The process began. I've written ten other books, but from the first moment I sat down in front of my computer, I knew this one was going to be different. The intensity of emotion and energy surging through my body was unlike anything I'd ever experienced before. It was as if thousands of ideas were all competing with one another to be the first to squeeze through my overheated brain and come to life on the page. I could barely hear myself think over the din they caused as each tried to make its point as loudly as possible.

But even more dramatic and challenging was something that became evident while I was writing my first chapter. Remember the flood in my house? I wrote about it at the end of chapter one, amazed that I had maintained my own state of inner happiness during such a disturbing crisis. I recall being amused and amazed that the universe had "tested me" and my principles before I was even twenty pages into the book. Well, my amusement turned into concern during chapter two, when the very issues I was presenting began to manifest in my life, and the concern turned into disbelief during chapter three (about change), when, naturally, everything that had seemed stable suddenly appeared to be completely uncertain.

I knew too much to pretend I wasn't aware of exactly what was taking place: I was being asked to fully experience each and every thing I was writing about *while* I was writing about it, and to practice every principle and technique I was offering you *while* I was offering it. In theory, this seemed very inspiring, but in reality, it scared me to death! After all, I knew what chapters were coming up: chapter four on obstacles, chapter five on the mind, and six on fear, just to name a few. "Oh, my God," I thought, "what is going to happen to me during each of these? How will I be tested? Will I survive this book?"

Now, I began to realize that I wasn't merely writing my next book—*I was being initiated into a new level of consciousness and that the book was my initiation rite.* I know about spiritual initiation. I have been privileged to undergo several of these life-transforming experiences over the past thirty years. So when I understood that this was, indeed, what was happening to me, I shifted from thinking I was working on the book to seeing it as a powerful process of meditation.

One day I had to fly to another city to give a lecture. I wasn't feeling very centered as I boarded the plane: I was worried that, perhaps, the book would be too challenging for me to write and I wouldn't be able to transcend the obstacles that kept coming up during each chapter to complete the manuscript in time to meet my deadline; and I still hadn't been able to figure out what Secret Number Ten was. It was in this state of mind that I found my seat and closed my eyes to meditate, hoping to find my way back to some peace.

For a while, I drifted between a quiet ocean of contentment and a turbulent sea of thought. Finally, I began to pray, listing all of my questions one by one: What should I do about a problem that had just erupted in my business? How should I handle someone from my past with whom I needed to complete a relationship? What could I do to stay calm while I waited for my house to sell? And of course, how was I going to figure out the tenth secret?

Suddenly, my body began to vibrate with a powerful energy. Waves of joy rose up within me, as if something wonderful had just taken place, and a deep feeling of peace filled my heart. Then, I heard a voice say very clearly:

"Whatever the question, love is the answer."

I gasped. This phrase exploded inside of my head like an orgasm of revelation: *Whatever the question, love is the answer.* What did it mean? Over and over, the phrase repeated itself, like the most jubilant of mantras. And each time I heard it, my awareness drank it in more deeply, until a moment came when, effortlessly, I knew what it meant.

Whatever the question, love is the answer. Whatever my worries, whatever my challenges, I needed to bring love to them. The solution somehow would contain love. The answer somehow would contain love. If I could bring love to each situation, I would find my way through it. If I could bring love to each situation, I would be free.

And then I knew that I'd not only been given the answer to my prayers, but I'd been shown the tenth secret.

So this is our tenth and final principle about life:

SECRET NUMBER TEN:

WHATEVER THE QUESTION, LOVE IS THE ANSWER

No matter what I am faced with, no matter what you are faced with, the solution is love. Every true solution to every problem comes down to love—more love, not less love; more compassion, not less compassion; more acceptance, not less acceptance. *We are being asked to love ourselves no matter what we are going through, to love oth-*

*ers no matter how they challenge us, to love the situations
we're faced with no matter how much we feel like resisting
them. It is love that will be our secret doorway to contentment.*

If you read no other chapter in this book, if you used
none of the nine other secrets about life but you fully
embraced this one, you would be able to transform your
life. Learning how to look for love in all situations will
change your perception of the world. Learning how to
bring love to every encounter will change how you experience the people who cross your path. Learning how
to see yourself with love will create true inner peace.

Everything changed for me after that revelation on
the plane. I had been given a technique to help me get
through my initiation and I have used it every day since.
Each time I was unsure of what to do about something
occurring in my life, each time I didn't know how to deal
with my own fears or concerns, each time I was being
hard on myself, each time I was having a difficult time
with another person, I would ask myself:

How can I bring the most love to this situation?
How can I see the love in what is happening?

And each time, I would find the answers to these questions in my heart and navigate my way back to love.

Sometimes these questions would lead me to one of
the other nine secrets, to help me understand what was
happening so I could let go of any attitude that wasn't
loving. When I remembered that my obstacle was there to

teach me something, I could love it. When I remembered that the person behaving unfairly toward me was my teacher, I could love him. When I remembered to stop postponing loving myself and honor myself in the moment, I could love myself now. *When I remembered that everything and everyone was just God in disguise, I could find the love in spite of what appeared to be taking place.*

An amazing thing began to happen as I practiced this principle—I began to feel even more love growing inside of me. Here I was under enormous pressure, trying to finish this book, getting ready to promote another, selling my house, preparing to move into a new home, and sorting out my personal life, just to name a few things that were going on, and yet I was more content and full of love than I had ever been before.

**When we bring love to a situation,
we will end up experiencing more love.**

Whatever the question, love is the answer. Whatever the problem, love is the answer. At the end of a day, if you've manipulated and controlled and resisted and rejected and blamed, all to make yourself right, all to protect your ego, have you really won a victory? Have you really gained anything? *Have you made more love?*

Only when we love do we truly triumph. Only when we love do we truly become what God intended us to be. Love is the only solution that resonates with the highest purpose of life. And that's why it is always the right choice.

When you see things like this, you are seeing things through God's eyes. Gurumayi Chidvilasananda, a modern spiritual master in the ancient yogic tradition of India, says: "It is in the experience of Love that God lives. Love is the abode of God. Love for yourself, for others, for animals, air, trees, the planet. Love for the mere experience of loving. When you are loving, you bring yourself close to God. You know how God feels about the Universe, about you. You have entered God's abode."

In this way, love is the ultimate spiritual practice. You do not have to sell your possessions and retire to a monastery or a cave in India. You don't have to give up your worldly pleasures and responsibilities and focus only on transcendental achievements. You do not have to turn away from your humanity. You simply have to love.

Go Where the Love Is

If you desire an embrace just open your arms.
RUMI

When you feel your heart begging for more love, there is only one thing to do—love. When you see your wounded self weeping over the love it never received, there is only one thing to do—love. When you hear your soul calling for love like a thirsty traveler pleading for water, there is only one thing to do—love.

If your path is love, it will lead to love.
Love your past

by accepting and blessing it,
love your present
by surrendering to it and not resisting it.
This is the way to ensure
that you will experience love in your future.

Here is a technique for opening yourself up to love:

Whenever you are longing for love, first remember
that it is waiting inside you.

Then, turn your attention within and find whatever
spark of love you can—remember those moments in which you felt love, or think of those
experiences which bring out your love, or recall
someone who inspires you to love.

Find this ray of love in your heart, the spark of love,
and focus on it.

Feel love, and it will expand.

Bathe in love, and it will start to flow.

See love, even the tiniest bit of love, and it will
grow.

The love of God, unutterable and perfect,
flows into a pure soul the way that light
rushes into a transparent object.

The more love that it finds, the more it gives itself;
so that, as we grow clear and open,
the more complete the joy of heaven is.

> *And the more souls who resonate together,*
> *the greater the intensity of their love,*
> *and, mirror-like, each soul reflects the other.*
> DANTE ALIGHIERI

When you open yourself to living as a channel for love, amazing things begin to take place in your life. Things that were confusing become clear. People who were difficult either vanish or transform. Doors that seemed to be permanently closed, open. Doors you never saw before suddenly appear before your eyes. *Love, like light, illuminates all it touches and reveals what was once invisible.*

My friend Rabbi Irwin Katsof wrote a beautiful book with the renowned journalist Larry King called *Powerful Prayers*. I called Rabbi Katsof and asked him if I could share one of my favorite stories in the book with you, and he graciously agreed:

There is an old story of a farmer who had three sons. He wasn't sure which of the three should take over the farm and so he devised a test. He called his sons together and told each one to fill up a barn to the brim. Whoever would succeed in filling his barn to the fullest would be the right one for the job.

The first son thought long and hard and determined that paper would be the most compact substance with the least air space. He collected tons and tons of scrap paper and stacked it very tightly until the barn was full. The father was impressed. Hardly any air space remained.

The second son had an even better idea. He brought in wagonloads of sand and poured it in through a hole in the roof. It was a brilliant idea and the father was even more impressed.

The third son did something totally different. He went into the barn and came out a few minutes later, inviting the father in to come see how he had filled the barn. When the father walked in, he saw to his surprise no paper or sand or any other substance. Instead, in the middle of the barn stood a small candle, its bright light piercing the darkness and filling the entire barn with light.

L ove fills every empty space with its own brilliance. That is why when you choose love, you are choosing light over darkness and hope over fear.

Love is like a great, relentless light
illuminating whatever it touches,
kindling the light in each heart with its own.

The more you love,
the more you give others permission to do the same,
and this is how your love will heal the world.

· · ·

Falling In Love with Life

Life is so full of meaning and purpose,
so full of beauty—beneath its covering—
that you will find that earth but cloaks your heaven.
Courage, then, to claim it—
that is all.
But courage you have, and the knowledge that we are
pilgrims together,
wending through unknown country, home.

FRA GIOVANNI

Several months ago I was in my car waiting on a small street for the light to change from red to green so I could turn onto the main road. One minute passed, then two, then several more, and I began to grow impatient. "Why isn't this light changing?" I muttered to myself.

Five more minutes went by, and still the light was red. Now I was going to be late for my appointment. "This is ridiculous!" I fumed. "At this rate, I will be here forever."

Finally, out of pure frustration, I inched my car forward as far as possible, as if this action would somehow intimidate the light into changing. And to my great surprise, within ten seconds, it did!

As I turned onto the main street of the busy intersection, I suddenly realized what had taken place. The traffic light on the quiet street I'd come from was triggered by a sensor, only changing if it detected a vehicle waiting to cross. My car had been too far back from the corner to register and that's why the light hadn't changed. As soon as I moved closer, the sensor got the message that I was there and gave me the green light.

We know that the purpose of life is to grow and every moment contains a lesson. What was the lesson in this experience? I smiled as I thought about how obvious it was:

> If you don't get close enough to the intersection,
> the light doesn't change.
> If you don't go up to the edge of your problem,
> your problem won't move.
> If you don't get close enough to life,
> you will remain stuck where you are.

If I'd stayed back and watched the traffic go by and become more and more annoyed with my situation, I might have sat there all day. Only when I nudged myself right up to what it was that I wanted did things start to move. This is how it is in our lives—*when we hold ourselves back from fully living, from fully participating, we get stuck.* We wonder why we feel bored or depressed, why we've lost the passion for our relationships, for our work, for life itself.

Whatever the question, love is the answer. How can you make more progress in your life? *Love.* How can you rediscover your natural joy in being alive? *Love.* How can you remove the obstacles that are preventing you from moving forward in the direction you've been wanting to go? *Love*.

Living your life with love means beginning to treat your days the way you would treat a lover. It means embracing each moment fully, intimately, rather than holding back, keeping your distance, and being stingy with your passion. It means moving fully into each experience, opening yourself to it with enthusiasm, with commitment, just as you would open your heart to the one you love.

Do you want to have an experience of ecstatic love? Set aside one day and imagine that it is going to be your last day on earth. Decide that you will live it as if tomorrow you would no longer be here. When you wake up next to the person you love, tell yourself, "This is my last day with my beloved. I'll never get to hold him in my arms again." As you eat your breakfast, tell yourself, "I'll never taste the delicious sweetness of fruits again." When you look at a tree outside your window, remind yourself, "I'll never see the beautiful miracle of Nature again."

Imagine what would happen to your perception and experience of reality if you looked at each object and related to each person in this way. Maybe you'd actually become spiritually liberated on the spot! Maybe you'd see the astonishing abundance in your life for the first time. One thing is for sure—you would feel overwhelmed with love, love for everything and everyone.

This is the way a lover sees the world. Think back to a time when you first fell in love. Didn't everything seem more beautiful? Didn't colors seem somehow brighter, sunsets more glorious, the evening stars more brilliant? Of course, nothing on the outside had changed at all from before you met your sweetheart. What was different was *you*. Your love was enabling you to see the world with new, more appreciative eyes.

> When you are in love with life,
> you see the world
> through the eyes of a lover.
> Seeing with loving eyes
> means noticing the beauty in everything,
> marveling at the magic in every moment,
> and looking for the love in everyone.

The Magic of Your Own Love

If you look for magic to be unusual or bigger than
yourself,
you may never realize how very near it is.
It is your heartbeat, your breath, your vision, your voice.
DEBBIE BERROW

If you are a woman reading this, then you already know about the magic of your own love. As the chosen form through which creation gives birth to itself, as the soft voice through which life's nurturing and sustaining power so sweetly offers its embrace, as the compassionate eyes through which beauty is seen so readily, as the open heart through which so much is generously and unapologetically felt, women embody the most essential qualities of the loving universe. And that is our deepest mystery—that somehow, without our even understanding how or knowing why, we are connected to an inner world of richness and wonder, a world as foreign to many men as it is home to us, a world beyond what is visible and tangible, the world that is the realm of the spirit.

Perhaps for you, too, reading this book has been an initiation. This reunion with yourself is the true purpose of your journey here on earth. It is a sacred pilgrimage whose destination is your own heart, whose hidden treasure is your own love. As you find your way back to your own true home, your own inner abode, you discover a shelter from which anything and everything is possible, a temple in which you can remember who you really are, a storehouse of inner treasures where you go to receive the gift of your own magic, your own fullness, your own divinity. To open yourself to that sublime gift and to bring it back to share with the world—this is a woman's true and enduring offering of love.

Whatever is happening,
you can always choose love.
You are always free to love.
This is your greatest freedom,
one that no one can ever take away from you.

My dear,
When anything ever touches or enters your body
Never say it is not Me—for God is just trying,
For the Beloved is just trying, to get close.
HAFIZ

You are such a courageous soul. You have chosen the path of love. You have chosen to wake up from your dream of forgetfulness. You have chosen to remember who you really are. Keep your vision strong and know that love is always there, even when you can't see it. It is the healing hidden underneath your pain. It is the seed of hope planted within your despair. It is the longing for union cloaked in your loneliness. It is the soft voice that calls to you through the darkness, beckoning you forward.

This voice of love has always found me, even when I was sure I had lost it forever. There was a time, while on vacation one summer years ago, when I was experiencing so much emotional turmoil that I feared I was cut off from any sense of love, and even from God. I went for a walk around a small lake, and as I circled the still water, my mind was anything but calm, churning with fear and sadness. But then, I noticed something else pulsating within me, something I hadn't felt in a while. And all at once, the words of this poem came pouring forth from inside me. I sat down on the grass and scrawled the verses on the back of an envelope I had in my purse.

When I read what I had written I wept, for I knew it was a message that had come through me from my own true self. I would like to share it with you, so you, too, know that the voice of love will always find you, just as it is finding you right now.

Could It Be You

I.   Beneath my pain
     I see something shimmering.
       Could it be You?
       Could it be You?

     Beneath my fear
     I feel something unwavering.
       Could it be You?
       Could it be You?

     Beneath the loss
     Of all that I used to be,
       Something is calling,
       Calling me home.

     Beneath this dream
     Another dream beckons me.
       Could it be You?
       Could it be You?

II. Beneath my mind
     The silence reverberates.

Could it be Me?
Could it be Me?

Beneath the veil
Wise eyes look back into mine.
 Could it be Me?
 Could it be Me?

Beneath each face
I've worn that is shattering
 Something is waiting
 To speak my true name.

Beneath this dying life
Someone is being born.
 Could it be Me?
 Could it be Me?

III. *I feel a hand grasp mine*
As I start to fall.
 Could it be God?
 Could it be God?

I see a cave of Light
In the emptiness.
 Could it be God?
 Could it be God?

"What is all this, Beloved?"
I cry in despair.

>*Dare I believe*
>*The answer I hear?*

>*"Yes, it is Me.*
>*Yes, it is You.*
>*Yes, it is Us.*
>*Yes, it is God . . ."*

Could it be your own love that you have always been feeling calling to you from within?

You know now that it is.

Could it be God's love that has been reaching out toward you through each lover, each friend, each beloved one?

You know now that it is.

And could it be that your own love and God's love are one and the same?

You know now that they are.

So, this is really the eleventh secret: *It is all love.* Everything—you, and me, and all the other people in this world, and the mysterious dance we are all a part of— it is all love. There is nothing but love, and that love is nothing but the divine presence of God.

What is there to do then, but to love? Are you ready? Love is waiting for you, to embrace you, to dazzle you, to heal you, to enlighten you, to adore you, in so many miraculous and unexpected ways.

Jean-Pierre de Caussade, a French priest and poet of

the eighteenth century, passionately captures this invitation as I would want to offer it to you:

> *Come, then, my beloved souls,*
> *let us run and fly to that love which calls*
> *us.*
> *Why are we waiting?*
> *Let us set out at once,*
> *lose ourselves in the very heart of God*
> *and become intoxicated with His love.*
> *Let us snatch from His heart the key*
> *to all the treasures of the world*
> *and start out right away on the road to*
> *heaven.*

· · ·

Come, then, my beloved reader,
my dear traveling companion,
and celebrate your initiation into love.
Look inside your heart and rejoice—
what sweetness, what splendor, what light!
You are so very beautiful . . .

Thank you for giving me the privilege of sharing
my love with you through these words.